FROM MARX TO MAO TSE-TUNG

FROM MARX TO MAO TSE-TUNG

A Study in Revolutionary Dialectics

by

GEORGE THOMSON

They have completely failed to understand what is decisive in Marxism, namely, its revolutionary dialectics.

—*Lenin*

CHINA POLICY STUDY GROUP
LONDON

To the memory of
DOUGLAS GARMAN
(1903-1969)

MADE AND PRINTED IN GREAT BRITAIN BY
THE GARDEN CITY PRESS LIMITED
LETCHWORTH, HERTFORDSHIRE
SG6 1JS

Preface

This is a Marxist study of the Russian Revolution of 1917 and the Chinese Revolution of 1949, designed to demonstrate their unity and continuity as two successive stages in the world socialist revolution. Their common theoretical foundation is expounded by means of extensive quotations from the Marxist classics, especially the writings of Lenin and Mao Tse-tung. These enable the reader to follow the two revolutions through the minds of those who led them, and at the same time they provide him with an introduction to the basic principles of dialectical and historical materialism; for that theory can only be understood in the light of the revolutionary struggles out of which it has grown and in which it finds its fullest and clearest expression.

The book is dedicated to the memory of Douglas Garman, from whom I received my training in Marxism. As national education organiser of the British Communist Party (C.P.G.B.), he created a network of Party schools, attended by industrial workers from all parts of the country and tutored by himself and others whom he had trained in his superb method of teaching through controlled discussion. He gave up this work in 1950 owing to disagreements with the Party leadership over the revisionist line of the *British Road to Socialism*, which he opposed from the beginning. In that struggle he was defeated, but among those who passed through his Party schools there were many who, like myself, have never forgotten his lessons in revolutionary dialectics, and this has helped them to see where the revolutionary path lies today.

Birmingham, 1971   GEORGE THOMSON

Abbreviations

(For full particulars of the works cited see pp. 170-182)

HE   More on the historical experience of proletarian dictatorship.

LCW   Lenin, Collected works.

ME   Marx and Engels, Selected works.

MEG   Marx and Engels, The German ideology.

MEP   Engels, The peasant war in Germany.

MER   Marx and Engels, On religion.

MFE   Mao Tse-tung, Four essays on philosophy.

MQ   Quotations from Chairman Mao Tse-tung.

MSW   Selected works of Mao Tse-tung.

PR   Mao Tse-tung and others quoted in *Peking Review*.

SCW   Stalin, Works.

SL   Stalin, Leninism.

SMT   The Moscow Trial and two speeches by Stalin.

SP   Stalin, Economic problems of socialism.

Contents

vii

CHAPTER I

The Dictatorship of the Proletariat

The first step in the revolution by the working class is to raise the proletariat to the position of ruling class, to win the battle for democracy.

—*Communist Manifesto*

1. *Working-class Power*

Lenin wrote:

> Those who recognise only the class struggle are not yet Marxists. . . . Only he is a Marxist who *extends* recognition of the class struggle to recognition of the *dictatorship of the proletariat*. This is what constitutes the most profound distinction between the Marxist and the ordinary petty (as well as big) bourgeois. This is the touchstone on which the *real* understanding and recognition of Marxism should be tested. (LCW 25.411.)

Thus, the concept of proletarian dictatorship enters into Lenin's very definition of a Marxist. Accordingly, if we accept this definition, we too must use it as a touchstone to distinguish between the conflicting interpretations of Marxism that are current at the present day.

Class society rests on exploitation. The exploiters form the ruling class, the exploited the subject class or classes. The ruling class enforces its rule by means of the state, which is an organ for the forcible repression of one class by another. Its chief instruments are the army and the police:

> The distinctive feature of the state is the existence of a separate class of people in whose hands *power* is concentrated. (LCW 1.419.)

> According to Marx, the state is an organ of class *rule,* an organ for the *oppression* of one class by another; it is the creation of 'order', which legalises and perpetuates this oppression by moderating the conflict between the classes. (LCW 25.387.)

> A standing army and police are the chief instruments of state power. (LCW 25.389.)

Thus, every form of class society—slave-owning, feudal, capitalist—is a dictatorship of the ruling class. The form of state varies. In capitalist—that is, bourgeois—society it may be more or less democratic; it may allow for parliamentary elections based on universal suffrage; but it is still a dictatorship—'a dictatorship of the bourgeoisie masked by parliamentary forms' (LCW 30.100):

> Bourgeois democracy, which is invaluable for educating the proletariat and training it for struggle, is always narrow, hypocritical, spurious and false; it always remains democracy for the rich and a swindle for the poor. (LCW 28.108.)

Accordingly, while urging the workers to make full use of bourgeois democratic rights 'in the spirit of the most consistent and resolutely revolutionary democracy' (LCW 21.409), Lenin warned them that it was an illusion to suppose that they could win power by parliamentary means. This was the main issue between him and the revisionists of his day:

The most dangerous thing about the Berne International is its verbal recognition of the dictatorship of the proletariat.... Attempts are being made to recognise the dictatorship of the proletariat in words in order to smuggle in along with it the 'will of the majority', 'universal suffrage' (this is exactly what Kautsky does), bourgeois parliamentarism, rejection of the idea that the entire bourgeois machinery of the state must be destroyed, smashed, blown up. These new evasions, new loopholes of reformism, are most of all to be feared.

The dictatorship of the proletariat would be impossible if the majority of the population did not consist of proletarians and semi-proletarians. Kautsky and Co. try to falsify this truth by arguing that 'the vote of the majority' is required for the dictatorship of the proletariat to be recognised as 'valid'. Comical pedants! They fail to understand that voting within the bounds, institutions and customs of bourgeois parliamentarism is a *part* of the bourgeois state machinery that has to be broken and smashed from top to bottom in order to pass from bourgeois democracy to proletarian democracy. (LCW 29.510.)

It follows that all attempts to use the apparatus of the bourgeois state, which serves to protect bourgeois rights, for the purpose of abolishing those rights, are doomed to failure :

It is the greatest delusion, the greatest self-deception, and a deception of the people, to attempt by means of this state apparatus to carry out such reforms as the abolition of landed estates without compensation, of the grain monopoly, etc. This apparatus ... is absolutely incapable of carrying out reforms which would even seriously curtail or limit the rights of 'sacred private property', much less abolish those rights. That is why it always happens,

3

under all sorts of 'coalition' cabinets, which include 'socialists', that these socialists, even when individuals among them are perfectly honest, in reality turn out to be either a useless ornament or a screen for the bourgeois government, a sort of lightning conductor, to divert the people's indignation from the government, a tool for the government to deceive the people. . . . So it has been and so it always will be so long as the old bourgeois, bureaucratic state apparatus remains intact. (LCW 25.369.)

Consequently, the bourgeois state can only be overthrown by force. The dictatorship of the bourgeoisie must be replaced by the dictatorship of the proletariat :

The essence of Marx's theory of the state has been mastered only by those who realise that the dictatorship of a *single* class is necessary not only for every class society in general, not only for the *proletariat* which has overthrown the bourgeoisie, but also for the entire *historical period* which separates capitalism from 'classless society', from communism. Bourgeois states are most varied in form, but their essence is the same : all these states, whatever their form, in the final analysis are inevitably the *dictatorship of the bourgeoisie.* The transition from capitalism to communism is certainly bound to yield a tremendous abundance and variety of political forms, but the essence will inevitably be the same : *the dictatorship of the proletariat.* (LCW 25.413.)

The form in which this dictatorship emerged in Russia was one in which the proletariat, supported by the poor peasantry, seized state power from the feudal landowners and the big bourgeoisie or capitalist class (LCW 29.119).

In this way, having seized power, the proletariat abolishes bourgeois democracy and replaces it with proletarian democracy :

4

The proletariat takes power, becomes the ruling class, smashes bourgeois parliamentarism and bourgeois democracy, suppresses the bourgeoisie, suppresses *all* attempts of *all* other classes to return to capitalism, gives *real* freedom and democracy to the working people (which is practicable only when private ownership of the means of production has been *abolished*) and gives them, not just the right to, but the *real* use of, what has been *taken* from the bourgeoisie. (LCW 29.511.)

Thus, the dictatorship of the proletariat means democracy for the people and dictatorship over the capitalists :

Bolshevism has popularised throughout the world the idea of the 'dictatorship of the proletariat,' has translated these words from the Latin, first into Russian, and then into all the languages of the world, and has shown by the example of *Soviet government* that the workers and poor peasants, *even* of a backward country, even with the least experience, education and habits of organisation, have been able for a whole year amidst gigantic difficulties and amidst a struggle against the exploiters (who were supported by the bourgeoisie of the *whole* world) to maintain the power of the working people, to create a democracy which is immeasurably higher and broader than all previous democracies in the world, and to *start* the creative work of tens of millions of workers and peasants for the practical construction of socialism. (LCW 28.293.)

Simultaneously with an immense expansion of democracy, which for the *first time* becomes democracy for the poor, democracy for the people, and not democracy for the moneybags, the dictatorship of the proletariat imposes a series of restrictions on the freedom of the oppressors, the exploiters, the capitalists. We must suppress them in order to free humanity from wage slavery; their resistance must be crushed by force. (LCW 25.461.)

In 1949, led by the Communist Party and Mao Tsetung, the workers and peasants of China seized power by force of arms and established a people's democratic dictatorship, that is, a form of the dictatorship of the proletariat corresponding to the special conditions of China. It differs from the Soviet form in certain features, which will be discussed in the next chapter, but in essence it is the same:

Who are the people? At the present stage in China, they are the working class, the peasantry, the urban petty bourgeoisie and the national bourgeoisie. These classes, led by the working class and the Communist Party, unite to form their own state and elect their own government; they enforce their dictatorship over the running-dogs of imperialism—the landlord class and the bureaucrat-bourgeoisie, as well as the representatives of these classes, the Kuomintang reactionaries and their accomplices—suppress them, allow them only to behave themselves and not to be unruly in word or deed. If they speak or act in an unruly way, they will be promptly stopped and punished. Democracy is practised within the ranks of the people, who enjoy the rights of freedom of speech, assembly, association, and so on. The right to vote belongs only to the people, not to the reactionaries. The combination of these two aspects, democracy for the people and dictatorship over the reactionaries, is the people's democratic dictatorship. (MSW 4.417.)

2. Continuation of the Class Struggle

The class struggle does not cease after the overthrow of

the bourgeoisie. On the contrary, it persists for a long time and in many respects becomes fiercer :

> The abolition of classes requires a long, difficult and stubborn *class struggle*, which, *after* the overthrow of capitalist rule, *after* the destruction of the bourgeois state, *after* the establishment of the dictatorship of the proletariat, does not disappear (as the vulgar representatives of the old socialism and the old Social Democracy imagine), but merely changes its forms and in many respects becomes fiercer. (LCW 29.389, cf. SCW 13.357.)

During this period the dictatorship of the proletariat has to be maintained in order to suppress the continued resistance of the bourgeoisie, to transform the economic basis by replacing capitalist with socialist production, and to carry the revolution into the ideological sphere :

> The bourgeoisie in our country has been conquered, but it has not yet been uprooted, not yet destroyed, not even utterly broken. That is why we are faced with a new and higher form of struggle against the bourgeoisie—the transition from the very simple task of further expropriating the capitalists to the much more complicated and difficult task of creating conditions in which it will be impossible for the bourgeoisie to exist or for a new bourgeoisie to arise. (LCW 27.244.)

> This dictatorship presupposes the ruthlessly severe, swift and resolute use of force to crush the resistance of the exploiters, the capitalists, the landowners and their underlings. Whoever does not understand this is not a revolutionary, and must be removed from the post of leader or adviser of the proletariat.

> But the essence of proletarian dictatorship is not in force alone, or even mainly in force. Its chief feature is the organisation and discipline of the advanced

contingent of the working people, of their vanguard, their sole leader, the proletariat, whose object is to build socialism, abolish the division of society into classes, make all members of society into working people, and remove the basis for all exploitation of man by man. This object cannot be achieved at one stroke. It requires a fairly long period of transition from capitalism to socialism, because the reorganisation of production is a difficult matter, because radical changes in all spheres of life need time, and because the enormous force of habit of running things in a petty-bourgeois and bourgeois way can only be overcome by a long and stubborn struggle. That is why Marx spoke of an entire period of the dictatorship of the proletariat as the period of transition from capitalism to socialism. (LCW 29.388.)

The class of exploiters, the landowners and capitalists, has not disappeared, and cannot disappear, all at once under the dictatorship of the proletariat. The exploiters have been smashed, but not destroyed. They still have an international base in the form of international capital, of which they are a branch. They still retain in part certain means of production. They still have money, they still have vast social connections. Just because they have been defeated, the energy of their resistance has increased a hundred and a thousand fold. The 'art' of state, military and economic administration gives them a superiority, a very great superiority, so that their importance is incomparably greater than their numerical proportion of the population. (LCW 30.115.)

More recently Lenin's view has been reaffirmed by Mao Tse-tung:

The current great proletarian cultural revolution is absolutely necessary and most timely for consolidating

8

the dictatorship of the proletariat, preventing capitalist restoration, and building socialism. (PR 69-18.15.)

3. *The Ideological Struggle*

Both before and after the proletarian revolution the proletariat has to wage a continuous struggle against bourgeois, and particularly petty-bourgeois, ideology. The formulation of bourgeois ideas is mainly the work of bourgeois intellectuals, who play an important part in the ideological struggle, especially in revolutionary periods. At such times some of them, like Marx himself, 'go over to the proletariat', having 'raised themselves to the level of comprehending theoretically the historical movement as a whole' (ME 1.43, cf. LCW 5.375).

The special features of petty-bourgeois ideology arise from the status of the petty bourgeois as a small proprietor. As such, he has a vested interest in bourgeois society; but at the same time, being exploited by the big proprietors, he is in constant danger of being ruined and thrown down into the proletariat. Occupying as he does an unstable position between the two main contending classes, he tends to vacillate :

It is a truth long known to every Marxist that in every capitalist society the only *decisive* forces are the proletariat and the bourgeoisie, while all social elements occupying a position between these classes and falling within the economic category of the petty bourgeoisie *inevitably* vacillate between these decisive forces. (LCW 28.186.)

The petty bourgeoisie inevitably and unavoidably vacillated between the dictatorship of the bourgeoisie (Kerensky, Kornilov, Savinkov) and the dictatorship of the proletariat; for, owing to the basic

9

features of its economic position, the petty bourgeoisie is incapable of doing anything independently. (LCW 28.300.)

In between the proletariat and the bourgeoisie there is another class of people, who incline first this way and then the other. This has always been the case in all revolutions, and in capitalist society, in which the proletariat and the bourgeoisie form two hostile camps, it is impossible for intermediate sections not to exist between them. The existence of these waverers is historically inevitable, and unfortunately these elements, who do not know themselves on whose side they will fight tomorrow, will exist for quite some time. (LCW 28.471.)

In its struggle for the allegiance of the petty bourgeoisie the proletariat has to carry on the same struggle within itself; for it has itself evolved historically out of the petty bourgeoisie, urban and rural, and moreover is constantly increasing its numbers from the same source. The struggle against the big bourgeoisie takes the form of an open confrontation between capital and labour, but the struggle against petty-bourgeois ideology is largely a struggle within the ranks of the working class:

One of the most profound causes that give rise periodically to differences over tactics is the very growth of the labour movement. If this movement is not measured by the criterion of some fantastic ideal, but is regarded as a practical movement of ordinary people, it will be clear that the enlistment of ever larger numbers of new 'recruits', the attraction of new sections of working people, must inevitably be accompanied by waverings in the sphere of theory and tactics, by repetitions of old mistakes, by a temporary reversion to antiquated views and antiquated methods, and so forth. (LCW 16.347.)

Nowhere in the world has the proletarian movement come into being, nor could it have come into being, 'all at once', in a pure class form, ready-made, like Minerva from the head of Jove. Only through long struggle and hard work on the part of the most advanced workers, of all class-conscious workers, was it possible to build up and strengthen the class movement of the proletariat, ridding it of all petty-bourgeois admixtures, restrictions, narrowness and distortions. The working class lives side by side with the petty bourgeoisie, which, as it becomes ruined, provides increasing numbers of new recruits to the ranks of the proletariat. (LCW 20.252.)

All over the world, in every capitalist society, the proletariat is inevitably connected with the petty bourgeoisie by a thousand ties, and everywhere the period of the formation of workers' parties was attended by its more or less prolonged and persistent ideological and political subjection to the bourgeoisie. This is common to all capitalist countries, but it assumes different forms in different countries, depending on historical and economic factors. (LCW 20.268.)

This struggle within the working-class movement is a necessary preparation for the revolution, because in a revolutionary situation even those disagreements which had previously seemed unimportant may suddenly become crucial :

It is quite natural that the petty-bourgeois world outlook should crop up again and again in the ranks of . the broad workers' parties. . . . What we now often experience only in the domain of ideology, namely, disputes over theoretical amendments to Marx; what now crops up in practice only over side-issues in the labour movement, as tactical differences with the revisionists and splits on this basis—all this is bound to be experienced by the working class on an incomparably larger scale, when the proletarian revolution will sharpen all disputed issues, focus all differences on points of immediate importance in determining the conduct of the masses, and make it necessary in the heat of the battle to distinguish enemies from friends and cast out bad allies in order to deal decisive blows at the enemy. (LCW 15.39.)

After the revolution the proletariat must maintain its ideological struggle throughout the period of socialist construction for as long as small-scale production, which is the basis of petty-bourgeois ideology, continues to exist :

Unfortunately, small-scale production is still widespread in the world, and small-scale production *engenders* capitalism and the bourgeoisie continuously, daily, hourly, spontaneously, on a mass scale. All these reasons make the dictatorship of the proletariat necessary, and victory over the bourgeoisie is impossible without a long, stubborn and desperate life-and-death struggle, which calls for tenacity, discipline, and a single, inflexible will. (LCW 31.24.)

The abolition of classes means, not merely ousting the landowners and capitalists—that is something we accomplished with comparative ease; it means *abolishing the small commodity producers,* and they cannot be ousted or crushed; we must *learn to live* with them. They can, and must, be transformed and re-educated only by prolonged, slow, cautious organisational work. They surround the proletariat on every side with a petty-bourgeois atmosphere, which permeates and corrupts the proletariat, and constantly causes among the proletariat relapses into petty-bourgeois spinelessness, disunity, individualism,

12

and alternating moods of exaltation and dejection. ... The dictatorship of the proletariat means a persistent struggle—bloody and bloodless, violent and peaceful, military and economic, educational and administrative—against the forces and traditions of the old society. (LCW 31.44, cf. MSW 3.215.)

4. 'Left' and Right Opportunism

The principal petty-bourgeois trends in the working-class movement are, in the order of their development, anarchism, syndicalism, reformism, and revisionism.

Anarchism originated in Russia. One of its leaders, Bakunin, was an opponent of Marx in the First International. According to Marx, the state, as the instrument of class rule, will necessarily persist so long as society is divided into classes; and the task of the proletariat is, not to abolish the state, but to replace the bourgeois state with the proletarian state. Only in this way can the conditions be created for the ultimate disappearance of classes. According to Bakunin, the abolition of the state is the immediate task, which the workers are to carry out, not by forming a workers' party, not by political struggle at all, but by direct action. The anarchists failed to understand that the abolition of the state belongs to a future historical stage, which can only be reached through the dictatorship of the proletariat :

Anarchism is bourgeois individualism in reverse. Individualism as the basis of the entire anarchist world outlook.... Failure to understand the development of society—the role of large-scale production—the development of capitalism into socialism. Anarchism is a product of *despair*. The psychology of the unsettled intellectual or the vagabond, not of the proletarian. (LCW 5.327, cf. 25.484.)

Syndicalism is closely related to anarchism. The syndicalist, too, repudiates the dictatorship of the proletariat. He maintains that through the trade unions the workers can call a general strike, seize control of production, and so overthrow capitalism.

Reformism originated in Britain. The Fabians were a group of intellectuals and working-class leaders who provided a theoretical basis for the Labour Party. Their idea of the 'inevitability of gradualism' embodies the essence of reformism—the idea that capitalism can be transformed into socialism by a series of gradual changes, without any qualitative change, that is, without a revolution.

From Britain reformism spread to the continent, especially to Germany, where it took the form of revisionism. The founder of revisionism was Bernstein, who had at one time been a Marxist. He borrowed many of his ideas from the Fabians (LCW 37.281, cf. 12.370). Revisionism differs from reformism simply in that the reformist ideas are presented as amendments to Marxism. In Germany Marxism was too deeply rooted among the workers to be ignored, and therefore it was reinterpreted in such a way as to be emptied of its revolutionary content :

The Bernsteinians accepted, and accept, Marxism minus its direct revolutionary content. They do not regard the parliamentary struggle as merely one of the weapons particularly suitable for definite historical periods, but as the main and almost the sole form of struggle, making 'force', 'seizure', 'dictatorship' unnecessary. (LCW 10.249, cf. 19.300.)

But, after Marxism had ousted all the more or less integral doctrines hostile to it, the tendencies expressed in those doctrines began to seek other channels. The forms and causes of the struggle changed, but the struggle continued. And the second half-century in the existence of Marxism began—in the nineties—with the struggle of a trend hostile to Marxism within Marxism itself. Bernstein, a one-time orthodox Marxist, gave his name to this trend by coming forward with the greatest noise and the most purposeful expression of amendments to Marx, revision of Marx, revisionism. (LCW 15.32.)

'The movement is everything, the ultimate aim is nothing'. This catch-phrase of Bernstein's expresses the substance of revisionism better than many long disquisitions. To determine its conduct from case to case, to adapt itself to the events of the day and to the chopping and changing of petty politics, to forget the primary interests of the proletariat and the basic features of the whole capitalist system, of all capitalist evolution, to sacrifice these primary interests for the sake of real or assumed advantages of the moment—such is the policy of revisionism. (LCW 15.37.)

When the Russian Social-Democratic Party was reconstituted in 1903, there existed within it from the beginning two contrary trends—the revolutionary trend, represented by the Bolsheviks, and the opportunist trend, represented by the Mensheviks :

In the turbulent years 1905-07 Menshevism was an opportunist trend backed by the bourgeois liberals, which brought liberal-bourgeois tendencies into the working-class movement. Its essence lay in an adaptation of the working-class struggle to suit liberalism.

Bolshevism, on the other hand, set before the Social-Democratic workers the task of rousing the democratic peasantry for the revolutionary struggle, despite the vacillation and treachery of the liberals. (LCW 21.332.)

In speaking of 'opportunism' here, Lenin is thinking of reformism or revisionism—of the Menshevik tendency to 'tail' behind the bourgeoisie. In the same period the Bolsheviks had to combat 'adventurist' or 'anarchistic' tendencies—what Lenin called 'revolutionary adventurism' (LCW 6.186) or 'petty-bourgeois revolutionism' (LCW 31.32, 33.21). In fact, these two opposite tendencies, the opportunist and the anarchist, are complementary to one another, like the two sides of the same coin :

> The anarchists rail at the Social-Democratic members of parliament and refuse to have anything to do with them, refuse to do anything to develop a proletarian party, a proletarian policy, and proletarian members of parliament. And in practice the anarchists' phrase-mongering converts them into the truest accomplices of opportunism, into the reverse side of opportunism. (LCW 15.391.)

> Anarchism was not infrequently a kind of penalty for the opportunist sins of the working-class movement. The two monstrosities complemented each other. (LCW 31.32.)

Thus, we may say that anarchism and reformism (or opportunism) are two petty-bourgeois tendencies in the working-class movement, which, although opposed to one another, are at the same time united in being both opposed to Marxism. In order to give expression to this underlying unity, Mao Tse-tung employs the term 'opportunism' to cover both tendencies and distinguishes them as 'Left' opportunism (anarchism and syndicalism) and Right opportunism (reformism and revisionism) respectively :

> History tells us that correct political and military lines do not emerge and develop spontaneously and tranquilly, but only in the course of struggle. These

16

lines must combat 'Left' opportunism on the one hand and Right opportunism on the other. Without combating and overcoming these harmful tendencies, which damage the revolution and the revolutionary war, it would be impossible to establish a correct line and win victory in this war. (MSW 1.194.)

Within the Party opportunist tendencies manifest themselves commonly in two forms : timidity, or 'tailism', due to over-estimation of the enemy, and impetuosity, or 'adventurism', due to under-estimation of the enemy. The Right opportunist tends to lag behind, the 'Left' opportunist to rush ahead :

> It often happens that thinking lags behind reality; this is because man's cognition is limited by numerous social conditions. We are opposed to diehards in the revolutionary ranks, whose thinking fails to advance with changing objective circumstances and has manifested itself historically as Right opportunism. These people fail to see that the struggle of opposites has already pushed the objective process forward, while their knowledge has stopped at the old stage. This is characteristic of the thinking of all diehards. . . .
>
> We are opposed to 'Left' phrase-mongering. The thinking of 'Leftists' outstrips a given stage of development of the objective process; some regard their fantasies as truth, while others strain to realise in the present an ideal that can only be realised in the future. They alienate themselves from the current practice of the majority of the people and from the realities of the day, and show themselves adventurist in their actions. (MSW 1.306, cf. 4.182.)

To sum up, we may say that there is only one road to socialism—the road that leads to and through the dictatorship of the proletariat. The opportunist road that is presented as an alternative, whether Right or 'Left', is in reality identical with the capitalist road, that is, the dictatorship of the bourgeoisie :

The main thing that socialists fail to understand and that constitutes their short-sightedness in matters of theory and their political betrayal of the proletariat is that in capitalist society, whenever there is any serious aggravation of the class struggle intrinsic to that society, there can be no alternative but the dictatorship of the bourgeoisie or the dictatorship of the proletariat. Dreams of some third way are reactionary, petty-bourgeois lamentations. That is borne out by more than a century of development of bourgeois democracy and the working-class movement in all the advanced countries, and notably by the experience of the past five years. It is also borne out by the whole science of political economy, by the entire content of Marxism, which reveals the economic inevitability, wherever commodity economy prevails, of the dictatorship of the bourgeoisie, which can only be replaced by the class which the very growth of capitalism develops, multiplies, welds together and strengthens, that is, the proletariat. (LCW 28.463.)

CHAPTER II

From the Bourgeois to the Proletarian Revolution

The development of modern industry cuts from under its feet the very foundation on which the bourgeoisie produces and appropriates products. What the bourgeoisie produces above all, therefore, is its own grave-diggers. Its fall and the victory of the proletariat are equally inevitable.

—Communist Manifesto

1. The Relation of Classes in Modern Society

The Russian Revolution of 1917 and the Chinese Revolution of 1949 are two successive events in a single historical process, which had its roots in the beginnings of capitalist society. In order to understand the relation between them we must see them both in relation to the process as a whole.

In his treatise *On Contradiction* Mao Tse-tung writes :

The fundamental contradiction in the process of development of a thing and the essence of the process determined by this fundamental contradiction will not disappear until the process is completed; but in a lengthy process the conditions usually differ at each stage. The reason is that, although the nature of the fundamental contradiction in the process of development of a thing and

19

the essence of the process remain unchanged, the fundamental contradiction becomes more and more intensified as it passes from one stage to another in the lengthy process. In addition, among the numerous major and minor contradictions which are determined or influenced by the fundamental contradiction, some become intensified, some are temporarily or partially resolved or mitigated, and some new ones emerge; hence the process is marked by stages. If people do not pay attention to the stages in the process of development of a thing, they cannot deal with its contradictions properly. (MSW 1.325.)

In human history antagonism between classes exists as a particular manifestation of the struggle of opposites. Consider the contradiction between the exploiting and the exploited classes. Such contradictory classes coexist for a long time in the same society, be it slave society, feudal society, or capitalist society; but it is not until the contradiction between the two classes develops to a certain stage that it assumes the form of open antagonism and develops into revolution. (MSW 1.343.)

Capitalist society rests on the growth of commodity production. It marks the stage at which labour-power itself has become a commodity. This is the essence of the process. Its evolution is determined by the development of the fundamental contradiction inherent in it, namely, the contradiction between the social character of production and the private character of ownership. This contradiction manifests itself in the class struggle between the proletariat and the bourgeoisie.

Feudal society evolves on the basis of a simple agrarian economy. The best part of the land is owned by the feudal lords and cultivated for them by peasants or serfs, who own their own implements but are obliged to hand over to their lords a portion of what they produce. The antagonism between these two classes is the principal contradiction of feudal society. As commodity production develops, there emerge, within the feudal system, two new classes—the bourgeoisie, or capitalists, engaged in trade and manufacture, and the proletariat, drawn mostly from the impoverished peasantry, who own nothing but their labour-power, which they sell to the capitalists in return for wages. Thus, the bourgeoisie finds itself in opposition both to the feudal lords, who obstruct the growth of commodity production, and to the proletariat, whose labour it exploits. This dual character—revolutionary in relation to the feudalists, counter-revolutionary in relation to the proletariat—is inherent in the nature of the bourgeoisie. In the final stage of feudal society the bourgeoisie places itself at the head of the peasantry and the proletariat and with their support overthrows the feudal lords and establishes itself as the ruling class. This is the bourgeois revolution.

In capitalist society commodity production is freed from all feudal restrictions. The feudal lords merge with the bourgeoisie, while the peasantry becomes differentiated into a rural bourgeoisie (farmers) and a rural proletariat (farm labourers). The principal contradiction is now the growing antagonism between the bourgeoisie and the proletariat.

Capitalist society develops through two main stages—industrial capitalism and monopoly capitalism or imperialism. Both stages are marked by further growth of commodity production and intensification of the antagonism between the bourgeoisie and the proletariat. In the first stage, based on free competition and colonial expansion, there emerge new contradictions—between the big bourgeoisie and the petty bourgeoisie, urban and rural, and between capitalism and the colonial peoples. These conditions lead to the second stage, marked by the transformation of free competition into monopoly, the export of capital, and the exploitation of the colonies as sources of cheap labour and raw materials. This stage is marked by intensification of all the major contradictions—between the proletariat and the bourgeoisie, between imperialism and the colonial peoples, and between rival imperialist powers; and these contradictions lead to imperialist wars, until in one country after another the proletariat seizes power with the support of the masses of the peasantry and establishes itself as the ruling class. This is the proletarian revolution.

The principal bourgeois revolutions of modern Europe are the English (1649), the French (1789), the German (1848), and the Russian (1905, 1917). In 1649 and 1789 the bourgeoisie seized power from the feudalists, but subsequently came to terms with them. In 1848 and 1905 it did not seize power but received certain concessions. In February 1917 it did seize power but was overthrown nine months later by the proletariat.

The hesitancy of the bourgeoisie in carrying through these revolutions arises from its dual character. If we examine them in turn, we find that each of them, as compared with the preceding, is marked by deeper contradictions, which lead gradually to a transformation in the character of the revolution. In 1649 the proletariat played only a very small part. In 1789 it was active but still dependent on the petty bourgeoisie. In 1848 it was so active that the bourgeoisie took fright and capitulated to the feudalists, leaving the revolution uncompleted. The same thing happened in 1905, only by this time the proletariat was so strong that a few years later it succeeded in forcing the bourgeois revolution through to its completion by carrying it forward into the proletarian revolution.

At the beginning of 1905, arguing against those petty-bourgeois socialists who disdained the idea of participating in a bourgeois revolution, Lenin wrote :

> To the proletarian the struggle for political liberty and a democratic republic in a bourgeois society is only one of the necessary stages in the struggle for the social revolution that will overthrow the bourgeois system. Strictly differentiating between stages that are essentially different, soberly examining the conditions under which they manifest themselves, does not at all mean indefinitely postponing one's ultimate aim or slowing down one's progress in advance. On the contrary, it is for the purpose of accelerating the advance and achieving the ultimate aim as quickly and securely as possible that it is necessary to understand the relation of classes in modern society. (LCW 8.24, cf. 9.50.)

2. *The Russian Revolution*

By the end of the nineteenth century the bourgeois revolutions of Western Europe had for the most part been completed. Feudalism had been abolished and capitalism was entering on the stage of imperialism. Russia, however, was still semi-feudal.

The growth of industrial capitalism in Russia may be dated from the Peasant Reform of 1861. This was a concession won by the new manufacturing bourgeoisie from the Tsarist autocracy, the regime of the feudal landowners. Its effect was to abolish serfdom in such a way that the landowners retained many of their feudal privileges, which they used to intensify their exploitation of the peasantry (LCW 17.121). Based on small holdings and primitive instruments, agriculture remained backward and unproductive. Famine was endemic. Many ruined peasants left their villages to work on the railways or to provide cheap labour for the new industries in the towns (LCW 2.99-100). Civil and political liberties did not exist (LCW 17.121).

The Peasant Reform was followed by a period of extremely rapid industrial growth :

> After 1861 capitalism developed in Russia so rapidly that in a few decades it brought about a transformation which had taken centuries in some of the old countries of Europe. (LCW 17.122.)

Hence, while the peasantry was crushed 'by innumerable survivals of medievalism as well as by capitalism' (LCW 18.143), the bourgeoisie found itself confronted, on the one hand, by an oppressive and corrupt autocracy, still obstructing the development of capitalism, and, on the other, by a vigorous industrial proletariat equipped with a knowledge of Marxist theory, which embodied the lessons learnt from 1789 and 1848 and also from the Paris Commune of 1871 (LCW 19.539-40).

These contradictions issued in the revolution of 1905. If the bourgeoisie had then placed itself at the head of the proletariat and the peasantry, it would have been strong enough to overthrow the Tsar and establish a bourgeois-democratic republic. But it shrank from doing so, because it was afraid of the proletariat :

> The antagonism between the proletariat and the bourgeoisie is much deeper with us than it was in 1789, 1848, or 1871; hence the bourgeoisie will be more afraid of the *proletarian* revolution and will

24

•   •

throw itself more readily into the arms of reaction. (LCW 8.258.)

Hence the bourgeoisie strives to put an end to the bourgeois revolution half-way from its destination, when freedom has been only half won, by a deal with the old authorities and the landlords. This striving is grounded in the class interests of the bourgeoisie. In the German bourgeois revolution of 1848 it was manifested so clearly that the Communist Marx spearheaded proletarian policy against the 'compromising' (Marx's expression) liberal bourgeoisie. Our Russian bourgeoisie is still more cowardly, and our proletariat far more class-conscious and better organised than was the German proletariat in 1848. In our country the full victory of the bourgeois-democratic movement is possible only in spite of the 'compromising' liberal bourgeoisie, only in the event of the mass of the democratic peasantry following the proletariat in the struggle for full freedom and all the land. (LCW 12.335.)

Accordingly, the bourgeoisie renounced its revolutionary aims and came to terms with the autocracy. The contradiction between feudal privilege and capitalist enterprise remained unresolved (LCW 13.442, 18.143, 20.375). Meanwhile, the monopoly capitalists of the West, who had already begun to invest in Russian industry, were supporting the Tsar, because they too were afraid of the proletariat :

The world bourgeoisie is giving billions in loans to an obviously bankrupt Tsar, not only because it is lured, like all moneylenders, by the prospect of big profits, but because it realises its own vested interest in the victory of the old regime over the

25

revolution in Russia, since it is the proletariat that is at the head of this revolution. (LCW 13.434.)

From the experience of 1905 Lenin concluded that the bourgeois revolution could not succeed in Russia so long as it was under the leadership of the bourgeoisie :

> In the view of the Bolsheviks the proletariat has laid upon it the task of pursuing the bourgeois-democratic revolution to its consummation and of being its leader. This is only possible if the proletariat is able to carry with it the masses of the democratic petty bourgeoisie, especially of the peasantry, in the struggle against the autocracy and the treacherous liberal bourgeoisie. (LCW 12.490.)

> The victory of the bourgeois revolution in our country is impossible *as the victory of the bourgeoisie*. This sounds paradoxical, but it is a fact. The preponderance of the peasant population, its terrible oppression by the semi-feudal big landowning system, the strength and class-consciousness of the proletariat, already organised in a socialist party—all these circumstances impart to *our* bourgeois revolution a *specific* character. This peculiarity does not eliminate the bourgeois character of the revolution. . . . It only determines the counter-revolutionary character of our bourgeoisie and the necessity of a dictatorship of the proletariat and the peasantry for victory in *such* a revolution. (LCW 15.56.)

Accordingly, Lenin put forward the perspective of a revolution to be effected in two stages : first, a revolutionary-democratic dictatorship of the proletariat and the peasantry, and, second, a dictatorship of the proletariat supported by the poor peasantry. In the first stage, the bourgeois-democratic revolution would be completed by abolishing the remnants of feudalism; in the second, the struggle for socialism would begin. By distinguishing the two stages in this way, the proletariat would gain the support of the whole peasantry for the first stage and ensure the continued support of the poor peasantry for the second. At the same time, while insisting on the need to distinguish between them, Lenin recognised that in the actual struggle the two stages might become interwoven, and in that case the proletariat should be prepared to pass without a pause from the first stage to the second :

The major distinguishing feature of this revolution is the acuteness of the agrarian question. It is much more acute in Russia than in any other country in similar conditions. The so-called Peasant Reform of 1861 was carried out so inconsistently and so undemocratically that the principal foundations of feudal landlord domination remained unshaken. For this reason, the agrarian question, that is, the struggle of the peasants against the landowners for the land, proved one of the touchstones of the present revolution. . . .

Such an alignment of forces leads inevitably to the conclusion that the bourgeoisie can be neither the motive force nor the leader in the revolution. Only the proletariat is capable of consummating the revolution, that is, of achieving complete victory. But this victory can be achieved only if the proletariat succeeds in getting a large section of the peasantry to follow its lead. The victory of the present revolution in Russia is possible only as the revolutionary-democratic dictatorship of the proletariat and the peasantry. (LCW 12.458.)

27

With all the peasants right through to the end of the bourgeois-democratic revolution; and with the poor, the proletarian and semi-proletarian, section of the peasants forward to the socialist revolution! That has been the policy of the Bolsheviks, and it is the only Marxist policy. (LCW 28.310.)

Like everything else in the world, the revolutionary-democratic dictatorship of the proletariat and the peasantry has a past and a future. Its past is autocracy, serfdom, monarchy, and privilege. In the struggle against this past ... a 'single will' of the proletariat and the peasantry is possible, for here there is a unity of interests.

Its future is the struggle against private property, the struggle of the wage-earner against the employer, the struggle for socialism. Here singleness of will is impossible. Here the path before us lies not from autocracy to a republic but from a petty-bourgeois democratic republic to socialism.

Of course, in actual historical circumstances, the elements of the past become interwoven with those of the future; the two paths cross. ... We all counterpose bourgeois revolution and socialist revolution; we all insist on the absolute necessity of strictly distinguishing between them. However, can it be denied that in the course of history individual, particular elements of the two revolutions become interwoven? (LCW 9.84-5.)

From the democratic revolution we shall at once, and precisely in accordance with the measure of our strength, the strength of the class-conscious, organised proletariat, begin to pass to the socialist revolution. We stand for uninterrupted revolution. We shall not stop half-way. (LCW 9.236-7.)

In February 1917, after two and a half years of imperialist war, the workers, peasants and soldiers of Russia were in revolt, demanding peace, land and bread. Isolated and utterly discredited, the Tsarist autocracy had opened secret negotiations with Germany for a separate peace. Then, under pressure from the British and French, who were determined to keep Russia in the war, the bourgeois leaders compelled the Tsar to abdicate and proclaimed a democratic republic. In this, however, they were acting from weakness, not from strength. It became clear that they had no intention of meeting the people's demands. Lenin perceived that, if what had been gained was not to be lost, it was necessary to pass at once to the second stage of the revolution :

> The specific feature of the present situation in Russia is that the country is *passing* from the first stage of the revolution—which, owing to the insufficient class-consciousness and organisation of the proletariat, placed power in the hands of the bourgeoisie—to its *second* stage, which must place power in the hands of the proletariat and the poorest section of the peasants. (LCW 24.22.)

> The question is one of advance or retreat. No one can stand still in a revolution. . . . Power transferred to the revolutionary proletariat, supported by the poor peasants, means transition to a revolutionary struggle for peace in the surest and least painful forms ever known to mankind. . . . (LCW 25.28.)

A year later, looking back on the October Revolution, Lenin wrote :

> The course taken by the revolution has confirmed the correctness of our reasoning. *First*, with the

'whole' of the peasants against the monarchy, the landowners, medievalism (and to that extent the revolution remains bourgeois, bourgeois-democratic); *then,* with the poor peasants, the semi-proletarians, all the exploited, against *capitalism,* including the rural rich, the kulaks, the profiteers, and to that extent the revolution becomes a socialist one. To attempt to raise an artificial Chinese Wall between the first and the second, to separate them by anything else than the degree of preparedness of the proletariat, and the degree of its unity with the poor peasants, means to distort Marxism dreadfully, to vulgarise it, to replace it with liberalism. (LCW 28.300.)

Speaking on the fourth anniversary of the revolution, Lenin said :

The direct and immediate object of the revolution in Russia was a bourgeois-democratic one, namely, to destroy the survivals of medievalism and sweep them away completely, to purge Russia of this barbarism, this shame, and to remove this obstacle to all culture and progress in our country. And we can justifiably pride ourselves on having carried out that purge with greater determination and much more rapidly, boldly and successfully, and, from the standpoint of its effect on the masses, much more widely and deeply, than the great French Revolution over one hundred and twenty-five years ago. . . . We have *consummated* the bourgeois-democratic revolution as nobody had done before. We are *advancing* towards the socialist revolution consciously, firmly and unswervingly, knowing that it is not separated from the bourgeois-democratic revolution by a Chinese Wall, and knowing too that in the last analysis *struggle alone* will determine how far we shall advance, what part of this immense and lofty task we shall accomplish, and to what extent we shall succeed in consolidating our victories. Time will show. But we see even now that a tremendous amount—tremendous for this ruined, exhausted, backward country—has already been done for the socialist transformation of society. (LCW 33.51.)

3. *The Chinese Revolution*

In 1940 Mao Tse-tung wrote :

The first imperialist world war and the first victorious socialist revolution, the October Revolution, have changed the whole course of world history and ushered in a new era. It is an era in which the world capitalist front has collapsed in one part of the globe (one-sixth of the world) and has fully revealed its decadence everywhere else; in which the remaining capitalist parts cannot survive without relying more than ever on the colonies and semi-colonies; in which a socialist state has been established and has proclaimed its readiness to give active support to the liberation movements of all colonies and semi-colonies. . . . In this era, any revolution in a colony or semi-colony that is directed against imperialism, i.e. against the international bourgeoisie or international capitalism, no longer comes within the old category of the bourgeois-democratic world revolution, but within the new category. It is no longer part of the old bourgeois, or capitalist, world revolution, but is part of the new world revolution, the proletarian-socialist world revolution. (MSW 2.343-4, cf. SCW 10.244-55.)

At the beginning of the present century China was a semi-feudal, semi-colonial country, in which the masses of the peasantry were exploited by the feudal landowners and by a number of colonial powers, which had occupied the ports, seized control of the banks, and established a commercial network for plundering the country. In this they were supported by the rich merchants, moneylenders and financiers who constituted the big bourgeoisie—the comprador or bureaucrat capitalists. These two classes, the feudal landowners and the comprador bourgeoisie, formed the social base for imperialist oppression in China.

Between these two exploiting classes and the masses of the people stood the middle, or national, bourgeoisie. These were industrial capitalists whose efforts to build native industries were frustrated by feudalism and imperialism. From that point of view they were inclined to side with the people, but at the same time they were themselves exploiters, afraid of the proletariat, and so they tended to vacillate.

The only consistently anti-feudal, anti-imperialist classes were the peasantry and the proletariat. The vast majority of the peasantry were poor peasants, that is, rural proletarians and semi-proletarians. The industrial proletariat was small, but after the first world war, and more especially after the October Revolution, it grew rapidly in strength and influence :

> The modern industrial proletariat numbers about two million. It is not large because China is economically backward. These two million industrial workers are mainly employed in five industries— railways, mining, maritime transport, textiles and shipbuilding—and a great number are enslaved in enterprises owned by foreign capitalists. Though not very numerous, the industrial proletariat represents China's new productive forces, is the most progressive class in modern China, and has become the leading force in the revolutionary movement. (MSW 1.18.)

Thus, the peasantry constituted the main body, and the proletariat the leading force, of the revolutionary movement :

Only under the leadership of the proletariat can the poor and middle peasants achieve their liberation, and only by forming a firm alliance with the poor and middle peasants can the proletariat lead the revolution to victory. (MSW 2.324.)

In the period 1911-27 there were several revolutionary uprisings, all directed against feudalism and imperialism, but none of them were successful :

Strictly speaking, China's bourgeois-democratic revolution against imperialism and feudalism was begun by Dr Sun Yat-sen and has been going on for more than fifty years. . . . Was not the revolution started by Dr Sun Yat-sen a success? Didn't it send the Emperor packing? Yet it was a failure in the sense that, while it sent the Emperor packing, it left China under imperialist and feudal oppression, so that the anti-imperialist and anti-feudal revolutionary task remained unaccomplished. (MSW 2.243.)

The bourgeois-democratic revolution which started in Kwangtung had gone only half-way when the comprador and landlord classes usurped the leadership and immediately shifted it on to the road of counter-revolution. (MSW 1.63.)

These failures proved that the aims of the bourgeois-democratic revolution were unattainable under bourgeois leadership :

What is the nature of the Chinese revolution? What kind of revolution are we making today? Today we are making a bourgeois-democratic revolution, and nothing we do goes beyond its scope. By and large, we should not destroy the bourgeois system of private property for the present; what we want to destroy is imperialism and feudalism. This is what we mean by the bourgeois-democratic rev-

33

olution. But its accomplishment is already beyond the capacity of the bourgeoisie and must depend on the efforts of the proletariat and the broad masses of the people. (MSW 2.242.)

Accordingly, it was argued by Mao Tse-tung that the bourgeois-democratic revolution should be carried through by the proletariat with the support of all the other classes opposed to imperialism and feudalism, including the national bourgeoisie. This was a new type of bourgeois-democratic revolution, which he named 'new-democratic' in order to distinguish it from the old type. In 1939 he wrote :

What indeed is the character of the Chinese revolution at the present stage? Is it a bourgeois-democratic or a proletarian-socialist revolution? Obviously, it is not the latter but the former. . . . However, in present-day China the bourgeois-democratic revolution is no longer one of the old general type, which is now obsolete, but one of the new special type. We call this type the new-democratic revolution, and it is developing in all other colonial and semi-colonial countries as well as in China. The new-democratic revolution is part of the world proletarian-socialist revolution, for it resolutely opposes imperialism, i.e. international capitalism. . . . A new-democratic revolution is an anti-imperialist and anti-feudal revolution of the broad masses of the people under the leadership of the proletariat. Chinese society can advance to socialism only through such a revolution. There is no other way. (MSW 2.326-7, cf. 1.290.)

Such was the evolution of the people's democratic dictatorship which was established in China in 1949, marking the completion of the bourgeois-democratic revolution and the inception of the proletarian-socialist revolution. The Chinese people's democratic dictatorship is the dictatorship of the proletariat in a new form corresponding to the conditions prevailing in a semi-colonial country in the new era introduced by the October Revolution. It resembles the Soviet form in that it, too, is based on the worker-peasant alliance, that is, on the alliance of the proletariat and the peasantry under the leadership of the proletariat; but it differs from the Soviet form in that the basis of the alliance is broader, including as it does the entire peasantry and the national bourgeoisie. In China the contradiction between the proletariat and the bourgeoisie was handled in such a way that the national bourgeoisie accepted proletarian leadership in the new-democratic revolution of 1949. This was only possible because the proletariat was guided by Lenin's theory of uninterrupted revolution as applied to the concrete conditions of China by Mao Tse-tung.

CHAPTER III

The Proletariat and the Peasantry

All previous historical movements were movements of minorities, or in the interest of minorities. The proletarian movement is the self-conscious, independent movement of the immense majority. The proletariat, the lowest stratum of our present society, cannot stir, cannot raise itself up, without the whole superincumbent strata of official society being sprung into the air.

—*Communist Manifesto*

1. The Leading Role of the Proletariat

There is only one really revolutionary class in modern society :

Beginning with the *Communist Manifesto,* all modern socialism rests on the indisputable truth that the proletariat alone is a really revolutionary class in capitalist society. The other classes may and do become revolutionary only in part and under certain conditions. (LCW 6.197, cf. 16.356.)

It is important to understand how the proletariat has come to occupy this position.

The antagonism between the proletariat and the bourgeoisie expresses, as we have seen, the fundamental contradiction of capitalist society, namely, the contradiction between the social character of production and the private character of ownership. As capitalism develops, with small-scale production giving place to large-scale production, so the contradiction between production and ownership is intensified, until the system of private ownership is shattered and replaced by a system of public ownership, that is, socialism.

The unit of capitalist production is the factory, in which large numbers of workers are brought together. These workers own nothing except their labour-power, which they sell to the capitalists in order to live. Of all the workers they are exploited the most intensively; but, working as they do together, they are in a position to organise themselves in self-defence. They take a united stand against the common enemy, become class-conscious, establish trade unions, create an independent working-class party, and equip themselves with Marxist theory, which is itself a product of their struggle :

> The very conditions of their lives make the workers capable of struggle and impel them to struggle. Capital collects the workers in great masses in big cities, uniting them, teaching them to act in unison. At every step the workers come face to face with their main enemy—the capitalist class. In combat with this enemy the worker becomes a *socialist,* comes to realise the necessity of a complete reconstruction of the whole of society, the complete abolition of all poverty and oppression. (LCW 16.301, cf. 7.415.)

In its knowledge of capitalist society, the proletariat was only in the perceptual stage of cognition in the first period of its practice, the period of machine-smashing and spontaneous struggle; it knew only some of the aspects and the external relations of the phenomena of capitalism. The proletariat was then still a 'class-in-itself'. But, when it reached the second period of its practice, the period of conscious and organised economic and political struggles, the proletariat was able to comprehend the essence of capitalist society, the relations of exploitation between social classes and its own historical task; and it was able to do so because of its own practice and because of its experience of prolonged struggle, which Marx and Engels scientifically summed up in all its variety to create the theory of Marxism for the education of the proletariat. It was then that the proletariat became a 'class-for-itself'. (MSW 1.301, cf. 312.)

Thus, we may say that the proletariat assumes its leading role in virtue of its conscious identification with the principal aspect of the principal contradiction in capitalist society. It represents the long-term interests of humanity. Just as the bourgeoisie overthrew the feudal system, which obstructed the full development of the forces of capitalist production, so the proletariat overthrows the capitalist system in order to free the productive forces for the further development which will put an end to the division of society into classes and the exploitation of man by man.

2. *The Worker-Peasant Alliance*

In contrast to the proletariat, the peasantry is associated with small-scale production and private ownership:

> The worker owns no means of production and sells himself, his hands, his labour-power. The peasant does own means of production—implements, livestock, his own or rented land—and sells the products of his farming, being a small proprietor, a small entrepreneur, a petty bourgeois. (LCW 18.37, cf. 22.95.)

The peasants are a class of small proprietors. This class is far less favourably situated in regard to the struggle for liberty and the struggle for socialism than the workers. The peasants are not united by working in big enterprises; on the contrary, they are disunited by their small, individual farming. Unlike the workers, they do not see before them an open, obvious, single enemy in the person of the capitalist. They are themselves to a certain extent masters and proprietors. (LCW 11.394, cf. 29.365.)

Nevertheless, there are certain conditions, due to the uneven development of capitalism, in which the proletariat can win the masses of the peasantry to its side.

In Russia capitalism developed later than in Western Europe, and it developed all the more rapidly for that reason, being partly supported by Western capital. The result was that the antagonism between the proletariat and the bourgeoisie—the principal contradiction of capitalist society—entered the revolutionary stage before the antagonism between the peasantry and the feudalists—the principal contradiction of feudal society—had been resolved. The two contradictions became interwoven. In these conditions, faced with an alliance between the big bourgeoisie and the feudalists, the proletariat formed an anti-feudal alliance with the peasantry, thereby rallying the masses of the people to its side. This alliance between workers and peasants was the basis of the revolutionary movement:

The proletariat by itself is not strong enough to win. The urban poor do not represent any independent interests, they are not an independent force compared with the proletariat and the peasantry. The rural population has the decisive role, not in the sense of leading the struggle—that is out of the question—but in the sense of being able to ensure victory. (LCW 11.343.)

Only the proletariat can bring the democratic revolution to its consummation, the condition being that the proletariat, as the only thoroughly revolutionary class in modern society, leads the mass of the peasantry and imparts political consciousness to its struggle against landed proprietorship and the feudal state. (LCW 12.139.)

In China capitalism developed even later than in Russia. It evolved from the internal contradictions of feudal society under the impact of imperialist oppression :

Just as a section of the merchants, landlords and bureaucrats were precursors of the Chinese bourgeoisie, so a section of the peasants and handicraft workers were precursors of the Chinese proletariat. As distinct social classes, the Chinese bourgeoisie and proletariat are new-born, and never existed before in Chinese history. They have evolved into new social classes from the womb of feudal society. They are twins born of China's old (feudal) society, at once linked to each other and antagonistic to each other. However, the Chinese proletariat emerged and grew simultaneously not only with the Chinese national bourgeoisie but also with the enterprises directly operated by the imperialists in China. Hence, a very large section of the Chinese proletariat is older and more experienced than the Chinese bourgeoisie, and is therefore a greater and more broadly based social force. (MSW 2.310.)

In these conditions, faced with an alliance between the comprador bourgeoisie, the feudalists and the imperialists, the proletariat formed an anti-feudal, anti-imperialist alliance with the peasantry, thereby rallying to its side the masses of the people, including even the national bourgeoisie :

> The Chinese proletariat should understand that, although it is the class with the highest political consciousness and sense of organisation, it cannot win victory by its own strength alone. In order to win, it must unite, according to varying circumstances, with all classes and strata that can take part in the revolution, and must organise a revolutionary united front. Among all classes in Chinese society, the peasantry is a firm ally of the working class, the urban petty bourgeoisie is a reliable ally, and the national bourgeoisie is an ally in certain periods and to a certain extent. This is one of the fundamental laws established by China's modern revolutionary history. (MSW 2.325.)

The influence of the proletariat over the peasantry was enhanced by the fact that in China the peasantry had no political party of its own :

> As China has no political party exclusively representing the peasants, and the political parties of the national bourgeoisie have no thoroughgoing land programme, the Chinese Communist Party has become the leader of the peasants and all the other revolutionary democrats, being the only party that has formulated and carried out a thoroughgoing land programme, fought earnestly for the peasants' interests, and therefore won the overwhelming majority of the peasants as its great ally. (MSW 3.298.)

Hence, in China as in Russia, the worker-peasant alliance was the basis of the revolutionary movement :

> To sum up our experience and concentrate it in one point, it is : the people's democratic dictatorship under the leadership of the working class (through

the Communist Party) and based on the alliance of workers and peasants. (MSW 4.422.)

In both countries the proletariat was only a minority of the movement which it led; but, as Lenin observed, the strength of the proletariat is not to be measured by its numbers :

> The strength of the proletariat in any capitalist country is far greater than the proportion it represents of the total population. This is because the proletariat dominates the nerve centre of the entire economic system of capitalism, and also it expresses economically and politically the real interests of the overwhelming majority of the working people under capitalism. (LCW 30.274, cf. 3.31.)

Moreover, in both Russia and China, the proletariat, though small in numbers, was relatively free from the influence of reformism. Of the Russian workers Lenin said :

> In Russia we see a series of shades of opportunism and reformism among the intelligentsia, the petty bourgeoisie, etc., but it has affected only an insignificant minority among the politically active sections of the workers. The privileged stratum of factory workers and clerical staff is very thin in our country. The fetishism of legality could not appear here. (LCW 21.319, cf. 19.160.)

Mao Tse-Tung says the same of the Chinese workers :

> Since there is no economic basis for reformism in colonial and semi-colonial China, as there is in Europe, the whole proletariat, with the exception of a few scabs, is most revolutionary. (MSW 2.324.)

Thus, the decisive factor in the role of the proletariat is not its numerical strength but its political strength.

3. The Differentiation of the Peasantry

Before the Peasant Reform of 1861, the relations of production in the Russian countryside had been predominantly feudal. The unit of production was the village, or group of villages, which was economically self-sufficient. What the peasants produced was consumed either by themselves or by the landowners, to whom they were in bondage. If there was a surplus, it was disposed of in the local market. Many of the peasants were impoverished as a result of crop failures and debts.

With the rapid growth of commodity production after 1861, these relations were to a large extent transformed into capitalist relations, but at the same time the big landowners retained many of their feudal privileges, which thus became an obstacle to the further development of capitalism. At the beginning of the present century some 15 per cent of the rural population were rich peasants, that is, capitalist farmers employing wage-labour; some 65 per cent were poor peasants, that is, rural proletarians or semi-proletarians, who had little or no land and lived by selling their labour-power; and the remainder were middle peasants, that is, smallholders, who were being steadily driven down into the proletariat (LCW 6.389, 28.56).

All sections of the peasantry had a common interest in the complete abolition of feudal relations; but, along with this contradiction between the peasantry and the feudal landowners, there was a deepening cleavage within the peasantry itself, which, especially after 1905, was being rapidly divided into a rural bourgeoisie (the kulaks) and a rural proletariat (LCW 15.42). Accordingly, the Social-Democrats, the party of the proletariat, set itself the task of mobilising the entire peasantry in support of the bourgeois-democratic revolution and at the same time of convincing the poor and middle peasants that their long-term interests lay in joining forces with the industrial proletariat in the struggle for socialism:

The Social-Democrats have pointed out repeatedly that the peasant movement sets before them a twofold task. Unquestionably we must support this movement and spur it on, inasmuch as it is a revolutionary-democratic movement. At the same time we must unswervingly maintain our proletarian class point of view; we must organise the rural proletariat, like the urban proletariat, and together with it, into an independent class party; we must explain to it that its interests are antagonistic to those of the bourgeois peasantry; we must call on it to fight for the socialist revolution, and point out to it that liberation from oppression and poverty lies, not in turning several sections of the peasantry into petty bourgeois, but only in replacing the entire bourgeois system by the socialist system. (LCW 8.231, cf. 4.422, 9.237, 10.438.)

Every advance in science and technology inevitably and relentlessly undermines the foundations of small-scale production in capitalist society: and it is the task of socialist political economy to investigate this process in all its forms, often complicated and intricate, and to demonstrate to the small producer the impossibility of his holding his own under capitalism, the hopelessness of peasant farming under capitalism, and the need for the peasant to adopt the standpoint of the proletarian. (LCW 15.35.)

The proletarian says to the small peasant: You are semi-proletarian, so *follow the lead* of the workers; it is your only salvation. The bourgeois says to the small peasant : You are a small proprietor, a 'labouring farmer'. Labour economy 'grows' under capitalism as well. You should be with the proprietors, not with the proletariat.

The small proprietor has two souls : one is a proletarian and the other a 'proprietory' soul. (LCW 20.216.)

Turning to China, we find that, although individual cultivation had been established there much longer than in Russia, the relations of production remained predominantly feudal right down to 1949 :

Among the peasant masses a system of individual economy has prevailed for thousands of years, with each family or household forming a productive unit. This scattered, individual form of production is the economic foundation of feudal rule and keeps the peasants in perpetual poverty. (MSW 3.156, cf. 1.16.)

The following assessment of the peasantry was made in 1939 :

The peasantry constitutes approximately 80 per cent of China's total population and is the main force in her national economy today.

A sharp process of polarisation is taking place among the peasantry.

First, the rich peasants. They form about 5 per cent of the rural population (or about 10 per cent together with the landlords) and constitute the rural bourgeoisie. Most of the rich peasants in China are semi-feudal in character, since they let a part of their land, practise usury and ruthlessly exploit the farm labourers. But they generally engage in labour themselves and in this sense are part of the peasantry. The rich-peasant form of production will

45

remain useful for a definite period. Generally speaking, they might make some useful contribution to the anti-imperialist struggle of the peasant masses and stay neutral in the agrarian revolutionary struggle against the landlords. . . .

Second, the middle peasants. They form about 20 per cent of China's rural population. They are economically self-supporting . . . and generally they do not exploit others but are exploited by imperialism, the landlord class,' and the bourgeoisie. They have no political rights. . . . Not only can the middle peasants join the anti-imperialist revolution but they can also accept socialism. Therefore the whole middle peasantry can be a reliable ally of the proletariat and is an important motive force of the revolution. . . .

Third, the poor peasants. The poor peasants in China, together with the farm labourers, form about 70 per cent of the rural population. They are the broad peasant masses, with no land or insufficient land, the semi-proletariat of the countryside, the biggest motive force of the Chinese revolution, the natural and most reliable ally of the proletariat and the main contingent of China's revolutionary forces. (MSW 2.323.)

When we compare this analysis of the Chinese peasantry with Lenin's of the Russian peasantry, we see that in China the worker-peasant alliance had a broader basis, and that this difference was due to the emergence of a new contradiction—the contradiction between the Chinese people and imperialism. By placing itself at the head of the struggle against imperialism, the Chinese proletariat was able to effect a shift in the balance of class forces and so to isolate the main enemy in the countryside—the feudal landlords. It was able to do this because it was guided, through the Communist Party, by Lenin's theory of the worker-peasant alliance as applied to China by Mao Tse-tung.

4. *The Lumpen-proletariat*

Thus, the worker-peasant alliance consisted basically of an alliance between the industrial workers and the poor peasants, that is, between the urban and the rural proletariat and semi-proletariat. It remains to consider the lumpen-proletariat.

This section is composed of declassed and demoralised elements, not regularly engaged in production, unorganised and largely incapable of organisation. In the early days of the working-class movement, when the proletariat was still struggling to become conscious of itself as a separate class and to develop the solidarity and discipline necessary for the creation of trade unions, the lumpen-proletariat was more of a danger to the movement than a potential asset :

> The 'dangerous class', the social scum, that passively rotting mass thrown off by the lowest layers of old society, may, here and there, be swept into the movement by a proletarian revolution; its conditions of life, however, prepare it far more for the part of a bribed tool of reactionary intrigue. (ME 1.44, cf. 155.)

A similar warning was given by Lenin in 1918, when the Russian workers were struggling to reorganise production in the chaotic conditions created by the war :

> Undoubtedly, the war is corrupting people both in the rear and at the front; people working on war supplies are paid far above the rates, and this attracts all those who hid themselves to keep out

of the war, the vagabond and semi-vagabond elements, who are imbued with one desire, to 'grab' something and clear out. But these elements are the worst that has remained of the old capitalist system and are the vehicles of all the old evils; these we must kick out, remove, and we must put in the factories all the best proletarian elements and form them into nuclei of future socialist Russia. (LCW26.468.)

With this may be compared the following appraisal by Mao Tse-tung:

Apart from all these, there is the fairly large lumpen-proletariat, made up of peasants who have lost their land and handicraftsmen who cannot get work. These lead the most precarious existence of all. ... One of China's difficult problems is how to handle these people. Brave fighters but apt to be destructive, they can become a revolutionary force if given proper guidance. (MSW 1.19.)

China's status as a colony and semi-colony has given rise to a multitude of rural and urban unemployed. Denied proper means of making a living, many of them are forced to resort to illegitimate ones, hence the robbers, gangsters, beggars and prostitutes, and the numerous people who live on superstitious practices. This social stratum is unstable; while some are apt to be bought over by the reactionary forces, others may join the revolution. These people lack constructive qualities and are given to destruction rather than construction; after joining the revolution they become a source of roving-rebel and anarchist ideology in the revolutionary ranks. Therefore we should know how to remould them and guard against their destructiveness. (MSW 2.325.)

This more positive appraisal reflects the advance of

the world revolution. As imperialist exploitation becomes more intense, so the numbers of the permanently unemployed increase; but at the same time, as the revolutionary struggle grows, so too the international proletariat extends its influence among all those whom imperialism has made outcasts.

5. *The Proletariat in the West*

Since the growth of the proletariat is determined by the development of capitalism, and since capitalism is most highly developed in the advanced countries of the West, it is pertinent to ask, why is it that in those countries no proletarian revolution has yet taken place? In their early years Marx and Engels expected that the first proletarian revolution would break out in Germany, but this expectation was not fulfilled. The French workers did seize power in Paris in 1871, but they were unable to hold it. At the time of the October Revolution Russia was the most backward state in Europe. At the end of the second world war there were revolutions in several countries in Central Europe, but not in the West. China in 1949 was more backward than Russia in 1917.

This question needs to be considered in connection with the converse question, why did the Russian and Chinese revolutions take place as early as they did? The answer lies, as we have seen, in the uneven development of capitalism. In Russia and China the bourgeoisie was still struggling to shake off the shackles of feudalism at a time when the bourgeoisie of the West had entered the stage of imperialism. It was weakened still further in Russia by its dependence on Western capital (LCW 20.399) and in China by imperialist oppression. The proletariat, on the other hand, was strengthened in Russia by drawing on the revolutionary experience of the West, and

49

in China by the example of the October Revolution and the support of the Soviet Union. These external factors combined to intensify the internal contradictions and so to shift the balance of class forces in favour of the proletariat.

In the West, where the development of capitalism had begun much earlier, feudalism had been almost completely eliminated, and from the beginning the bourgeoisie had been enriching themselves from the plunder of America and Asia. In this way they strengthened their position at home. Drawing on the immense profits of colonial exploitation, they made substantial concessions to the industrial workers and bought over many of their leaders. Hence, in addition to the gulf dividing the proletariat of the metropolitan countries from the workers and peasants of the colonies, the metropolitan proletariat was itself divided and infected to a considerable extent with bourgeois ideology. The effect of imperialism in these countries was to mitigate the internal contradictions and so to shift the balance of class forces in favour of the bourgeoisie.

That this was Lenin's opinion is clear from many passages in his writings :

> Only the proletarian class, which maintains the whole of society, can bring about the social revolution. However, as a result of the colonial policy, the European proletarian finds himself *partly* in a position in which it is not his own labour, but the labour of the practically enslaved natives in the colonies, that maintains the whole of society.... In certain countries this provides the material and economic basis for infecting the proletariat with colonial chauvinism. (LCW 13.77, cf. 21.243.)

Is the actual condition of the workers in the oppressor and the oppressed nations the same, from the standpoint of the national question? No, it is not the same.

(1) *Economically* the difference is that sections of the working class in the oppressor nations receive crumbs from the *super-profits* which the bourgeoisie of those nations obtains by extra exploitation of the workers of the oppressed nations. Besides, economic statistics show that here a *larger* percentage of the workers become 'straw bosses' than in the oppressed nations, a *larger* percentage rise to the labour *aristocracy*. That is a fact. To a *certain degree* the workers of the oppressor nations are partners of *their own* bourgeoisie in plundering the workers—and the mass of the population—of the oppressed nations.

(2) *Politically,* the difference is that, compared with the workers of the oppressed nations, they occupy a *privileged* position in many spheres of political life.

(3) *Ideologically*, or spiritually, the difference is that they are taught, at school and in life, disdain and contempt for the workers of the oppressed nations. (LCW 23.55, cf. 22.283.)

It would perhaps be expedient to emphasise more strongly and to express more vividly in our programme the prominence of the handful of the richest imperialist countries, which prosper parasitically by robbing colonies and weaker nations. This is an extremely important feature of imperialism. To a certain extent it facilitates the rise of powerful revolutionary movements in countries subjected to imperialist plunder and in danger of being crushed and partitioned by the imperialist giants (such as Russia), and on the other hand it tends to a certain extent to prevent the rise of profound revolutionary movements in the countries that plunder by imperialist methods many colonies and foreign lands, and thus make a comparatively large portion of their population *participants* in the division of the imperialist loot. (LCW 26.168, cf. 29.123, 31.191, 230.)

However, in regard to Britain it must not be forgotten that . . . . the percentage of workers and office employees who enjoy a petty-bourgeois standard of living is exceptionally high, owing to the actual enslavement of millions of people in Britain's colonial possessions. (LCW 32.456.)

So we see that in the imperialist countries even the proletariat, that most revolutionary of classes, may cease to be revolutionary.

At the present day, with the oppressed peoples in revolt all over the world and imperialism heading for total collapse, the situation in the West is beginning to change. If the relatively high standard of living enjoyed by the workers of these countries was won on the basis of colonial exploitation, then, with the collapse of that basis, they will be compelled to shed their reformist illusions, and so will recover their revolutionary consciousness.

Finally, it may be noted that in these advanced capitalist countries the industrial workers form a higher percentage of the total population than in any others. Again we see that the strength of the proletariat is not to be measured by its numbers.

CHAPTER IV

The National Question

In proportion as the exploitation of one individual by another is put an end to, the exploitation of one nation by another will also be put an end to In proportion as the antagonism between classes within the nation vanishes, the hostility of one nation to another will come to an end.

—*Communist Manifesto*

1. *The Nation in Modern Society*

The nation is a social formation which first took shape with the growth of commodity production during the transition from feudalism to capitalism. One of the aims of the bourgeois-democratic revolution is national independence. In the evolution of capitalist society, a struggle for national independence—a national movement, as it is called—arises when the bourgeoisie of a subject people rallies the rest of the people in an attempt to shake off the rule of a foreign power and establish its own state. The word 'people' in this context means a community of persons occupying a common territory and speaking a common language. Such communities have, of course, existed from the earliest times, but it is only in modern society that they have become nations.

The economic basis of national movements was explained by Lenin as follows :

For the complete victory of commodity production, the bourgeoisie must capture the home market, and there must be politically united territories whose population speaks a single language, with all obstacles to the development of the language and its consolidation in literature eliminated. Therein lies the economic foundation of national movements.

Language is the most important means of human intercourse. Unity and unimpeded development of language are the most important conditions for genuinely free and extensive commerce on a scale commensurate with modern capitalism, for a free and broad grouping of the population in all its various classes, and lastly for establishing a close connection between the market and every proprietor, big and small, and between buyer and seller. (LCW 20.396.)

The earliest national movements arose in Western Europe. Out of the unstable, heterogeneous kingdoms of the feudal era there emerged, mainly in the seventeenth and eighteenth centuries, a dozen independent states. Most of these developed as single-nation states : that is to say, each country was occupied by a single people speaking a common language. Only in the British Isles was there a national minority large enough to give rise to a struggle for independence. The English failed to consolidate their conquest of Ireland, and during the eighteenth century there arose an Irish national movement.

It must be remembered, however, in speaking of these countries as single-nation states, that most of them were engaged from the beginning in carving out colonial empires overseas. In this way nations formerly oppressed became themselves oppressors of other peoples. The result was both to promote the growth of national movements among the colonial peoples and also, as explained in Chapter III, to retard the proletariat of the oppressor nation in its struggle against the bourgeoisie :

'No nation can be free if it oppresses other nations' (Marx and Engels). A proletariat that tolerates the slightest coercion of other nations by its 'own' nation cannot be a socialist proletariat. (LCW 21.317.)

Turning to Eastern Europe as it was on the eve of the first world war, we find that, outside the Balkans, where there were six small states (several of them with substantial national minorities), there were no single-nation states at all. The whole area was covered by two multinational states, feudal in origin and torn by national conflicts. At the end of the war the Austro-Hungarian Empire broke up into a number of independent bourgeois nation-states, and meanwhile the Russian Empire was transformed into a union of socialist republics with smaller autonomous areas inhabited by national minorities. Their line on the national question was an important factor contributing to the victory of the Bolsheviks in those areas (SCW 6.152).

To complete the picture, we must add two major nation-states from outside Europe.

The United States of America was formed from a group of colonies founded by West European settlers, who in 1776 declared their independence of British rule. Augmented continuously by mass immigration from all parts of Europe, the population has nevertheless (apart from the Negroes and the Indians) been unified on the basis of bourgeois equality and the use of a common language :

We know that the specially favourable conditions in America for the development of capitalism, and the rapidity of this development, have produced a situation in which vast national differences are speedily and fundamentally smoothed out, as nowhere else in the world, to form a single 'American' nation. (LCW 23.276.)

In Japan the development of capitalism was as late

as in Russia and so rapid that the bourgeoisie merged with the feudal nobility without a breach. Japan was the only nation-state of non-European origin to become a major imperialist power :

> In Asia itself the conditions for the most complete development of commodity production and the freest, widest, speediest growth of capitalism have been created only in Japan, that is, only in an independent nation-state. Japan is a bourgeois state, and for that reason has itself begun to oppress other nations and to enslave colonies. We cannot say whether Asia will have had time to develop into a system of independent nation-states, like Europe, before the collapse of capitalism; but it remains an undisputed fact that capitalism, having awakened Asia, has called forth national movements everywhere in that continent too. (LCW 20.399.)

Summing up the situation as he saw it in 1916, Lenin distinguished three types of national movement :

> First type : the advanced countries of Western Europe (and America), where the national movement is a thing of the *past*. Second type : Eastern Europe, where it is a thing of the *present*. Third type : the semi-colonies and colonies, where it is largely a thing of the *future*. (LCW 23.38.)

Finally, we must note that, in addition to the creation of separate nation-states, capitalism reveals, in its later stages, a contrary tendency leading to the removal of national barriers :

> Developing capitalism knows two historical tendencies in the national question. The first is the awakening of national life and national movements, the struggle against all national oppression, and the creation of nation-states. The second is the develop-

ment and growing frequency of international intercourse in every form, the breakdown of national barriers, the creation of the international unity of capital, of economic life in general, of politics, science, etc. Both tendencies are a universal law of capitalism. The former predominates in the beginning of its development, the latter characterises a mature capitalism moving towards its transformation into socialist society. (LCW 20.27.)

The international unity of capital calls forth the international unity of labour. After the contradiction between capital and labour has been resolved in socialism, national divisions will finally disappear :

> To the old world, the world of national oppression, national bickering, and national isolation, the workers counterpose a new world, a world of unity between the working people of all nations, a world in which there is no place for any privileges or for the slightest degree of oppression of man by man. (LCW 19.92.)

2. *National Self-determination*

The attitude of the proletariat to the national question follows from its attitude to the bourgeois revolution. The proletariat supports the bourgeoisie in its struggle against feudalism and imperialism, and is ready to take over the leadership of that struggle, if the bourgeoisie should capitulate. Accordingly, it supports the bourgeois-democratic principle of equal rights for all citizens, regardless of nationality, and recognises that nations emerging within a multinational state have the right to secede :

> For different nations to live together in peace and freedom, or to separate and form different states (if that is more convenient for them), a full democracy,

57

upheld by the working class, is essential. No privileges for any one nation or any one language; not the slightest degree of oppression or the slightest injustice in respect of a national minority—such are the principles of working-class democracy. (LCW 19.91, cf. 243.)

In so far as national peace is possible at all in a capitalist society based on exploitation, profit-making and strife, it is attainable only under a consistently and thoroughly democratic republican system of government which guarantees full equality for all nations and languages, recognises no compulsory official language, provides the people with schools where instruction is given in all the native languages, and has a constitution containing a fundamental law which prohibits any privileges to any one nation and any encroachment on the rights of a national minority. (LCW 19.427.)

At the same time, while supporting the bourgeois-democratic principle of equal rights for all nationalities, the proletariat insists, in opposition to the bourgeoisie, that the national struggle is subordinate to the class struggle :

The bourgeoisie always places its national demands in the forefront, and does so in categorical fashion. With the proletariat, however, these demands are subordinated to the interests of the class struggle. (LCW 20.410.)

Successful struggle against exploitation requires that the proletariat should be free of nationalism, and be absolutely neutral, so to speak, in the fight for supremacy that is going on among the bourgeoisie of the various nations. If the proletariat of any one nation gives the slightest support to the privileges of 'its own' national bourgeoisie, that will inevitably arouse distrust among the proletariat of another nation; it will weaken the international class solidarity of the workers and divide them, to the delight of the bourgeoisie. (LCW 20.424.)

The proletariat cannot support any consecration of nationalism; on the contrary, it supports everything that helps to obliterate national distinctions and remove national barriers; it supports everything that makes the ties between nationalities closer, or tends to merge nations. (LCW 20.35.)

If the proletariat favours the merging of nations, why, it may be asked, does it recognise their right to independence? Because it is only through the fulfilment of national aspirations that national divisions can be overcome :

We want *free* unification; that is why we must recognise the right to secede. Without freedom to secede, unification cannot be called free. (LCW 26.176.)

3. *Wars of National Liberation*

At the Third Congress of the Communist International (1921) Lenin said :

It is perfectly clear that in the impending decisive battles of the world revolution the movement of the majority of the world's population, directed initially towards national liberation, will turn against capitalism and imperialism, and will perhaps play a much more revolutionary part than we expect. . . . In spite of the fact that the masses of toilers—the peasants in the colonial countries—are still backward, they will play a very important revolutionary part in the coming phases of the world revolution. (LCW 32.482.)

Since then, throughout the colonial and semi-colonial world the class struggle has assumed the form of national struggle, giving rise to wars of national liberation and revolutions of the 'new-democratic' type discussed in Chapter II. In China during the war of resistance against Japan Mao Tse-tung said :

> In a struggle which is national in character the class struggle takes the form of national struggle, which demonstrates the identity between the two. On the one hand, for a given historical period the political and economic demands of the various classes must not be such as to disrupt co-operation; on the other hand, the demands of the national struggle (the need to resist Japan) should be the point of departure for all class struggle. Thus there is identity in the united front between unity and independence and between the national struggle and the class struggle. (MSW 2.215.)

It has recently been demonstrated in one country after another, and above all in Vietnam, that even a small and materially backward nation, organised under the Communist Party and guided by Mao Tse-tung's strategy of people's war, can defeat the most powerful of all imperialist states, armed with a vast military machine on which monopoly capitalism has squandered all its wealth.

The war of liberation in Vietnam has won world-wide support. In this way the national struggle of a single people has become an international struggle, which in its turn has aroused new national struggles in other countries, including the United States. The struggle of the American Negroes for freedom and equal rights is itself a national movement, as Lenin recognised :

> In the United States, the Negroes ... should be classed as an oppressed nation; for the equality won in the Civil War of 1861-65, and guaranteed by the Constitution of the Republic, was in many respects increasingly curtailed in the chief Negro areas (the South) in connection with the transition from the progressive, pre-monopoly capitalism of 1860-70 to the reactionary, monopoly capitalism (imperialism) of the new era. . . . (LCW 23.275.)

Similarly, in declaring his support for the movement, Mao Tse-tung has pointed out that it is both a national struggle and a class struggle :

> The speedy development of the struggle of the American Negroes is a manifestation of sharpening class struggle and sharpening national struggle within the United States. . . .
> In the final analysis, national struggle is a matter of class struggle. . . . The evil system of colonialism and imperialism arose and throve with the enslavement of Negroes and the trade in Negroes, and it will surely come to its end with the complete emancipation of the black people. (PR 63-33.)

As the struggles for national liberation expand, so the area remaining under imperialist rule contracts; as that area contracts, so its exploitation is intensified, thus provoking new struggles for national liberation. This is the vicious circle from which imperialism has no escape :

> U.S. imperialism, which looks like a huge monster, is in essence a paper tiger, now in the throes of its death-bed struggle. In the world of today, who actually fears whom? It is not the Vietnamese

people, the Laotian people, the Palestinian people, the Arab people, or the people of other countries, who fear U.S. imperialism; it is U.S. imperialism which fears the people of the world. It becomes panic-stricken at the mere rustle of leaves in the wind. Innumerable facts prove that a just cause enjoys abundant support, while an unjust cause finds little support. A weak nation can defeat a strong, a small nation can defeat a big. The people of a small country can certainly defeat oppression by a big country, if only they dare to rise in struggle, dare to take up arms, and grasp in their own hands the destiny of their country. This is a law of history. (PR 70-22.)

4. *National versus Regional Autonomy*

In affirming the right of every nation to secede and form an independent state, Lenin did not mean that the party of the proletariat was committed in all cases to advocating the exercise of that right. On the contrary, he recognised that in some cases secession might be inexpedient:

> The right of nations to self-determination (that is, the constitutional guarantee of an absolutely free and democratic method of deciding the question of secession) must under no circumstances be confused with the expediency of secession for a given nation. The Social-Democratic Party must decide the question exclusively on its merits in each case in conformity with the interests of social development as a whole and with the interests of the proletarian class struggle for socialism. (LCW 19.429.)

It may also happen, of course, that secession is precluded by the objective situation. Some nationalities are too small or too scattered to form independent states. How, then, is the national question to be solved in cases where secession is judged to be inexpedient or impracticable?

There are, as Lenin points out, two opposite solutions of this problem—the bourgeois solution of cultural-national autonomy and the proletarian solution of regional and local autonomy.

According to the principle of cultural-national autonomy, the members of each nationality form a 'national association', which controls their social and cultural life, including education. Thus, the schools are segregated according to nationality. Lenin asks:

Is such a division, be it asked, permissible from the standpoint of democracy in general and from the standpoint of the interests of the proletarian class struggle in particular?

A clear grasp of the essence of the 'cultural-national' autonomy programme is sufficient to enable one to reply without hesitation: it is absolutely impermissible. . . .

If the various nations living in a single state are bound by economic ties, then any attempt to divide them permanently in 'cultural' and particularly educational matters would be absurd and reactionary. On the contrary, efforts should be made to *unite* the nations in educational matters, so that the schools should be a preparation for what is actually done in real life. At the present time we see that the different nations are unequal in the rights they possess and in their level of development. Under these circumstances, to segregate the schools according to nationality would *actually* and inevitably *worsen* the conditions of the more backward nations. . . .

Segregating the schools according to nationality is not only a *harmful* scheme but a downright swindle on the part of the *capitalists*. The workers *can* be split up, divided and weakened by the advocacy of such an idea, and still more by segregation of the ordinary people's schools according to nationality; while the capitalists, whose children are well provided with rich private schools and specially engaged tutors, *cannot in any way* be threatened by any division or weakening through 'cultural-national autonomy'. (LCW 19.503-5.)

Thus, the effect of cultural-national autonomy is to divide the workers and so place them more firmly under bourgeois control.

Against this Lenin put forward the principle of regional and local autonomy. True national equality, he argued, calls for :

wide regional autonomy and fully democratic self-government, with the boundaries of the self-governing and autonomous regions determined by the local inhabitants on the basis of economic and social conditions, national make-up of the population, etc. (LCW 19.427.)

In order to eliminate national oppression, it is very important to create autonomous areas, however small, with entirely homogeneous populations, towards which members of the respective nationalities scattered all over the country, or even all over the world, could gravitate, and with which they could enter into relations and free associations of every kind. (LCW 20.50.)

The principle of local autonomy also includes :

the right of the population to receive instruction in their native tongue in schools to be established for the purpose at the expense of the state and the local organs of self-government; the right of every citizen to use his native language at meetings; the native language to be used in all local, public and state institutions; the obligatory official language to be abolished. (LCW 24.472.)

On the last point Lenin has also this to say :

The requirements of economic exchange will themselves *decide* which language of the given country it is to the *advantage* of the majority to know in the interests of commercial relations. (LCW 19.355.)

Is not an 'official language' a stick that *drives people away* from the Russian language? Why will you not understand the *psychology* which is so important in the national question, and which, if the slightest coercion is applied, besmirches, soils, nullifies the undoubtedly progressive importance of centralisation, large states, and a uniform language? (LCW 19.499.)

There still remains the problem of the large industrial centres, whose population is necessarily heterogeneous, being drawn from all parts of the country and from countries overseas, and is at the same time so closely mixed that even the principle of local autonomy is insufficient to ensure full national equality. This was already a world-wide problem in Lenin's time :

There can be no doubt that dire poverty alone compels people to abandon their native land, and that the capitalists exploit the immigrant workers in the most shameless manner. But only reactionaries can shut their eyes to the *progressive* significance of this modern migration of nations. (LCW 19.454.)

Referring to the school census of 1911, Lenin remarks :

The extremely mixed national composition of the population of the large city of St. Petersburg is at once evident. This is no accident but results from a *law* of capitalism, which operates in all continents and in all parts of the world. Large cities, factory centres, railway centres, commercial and industrial centres generally, are certain, more than any others, to have very mixed populations, and it is precisely these centres that grow faster than others and attract ever larger numbers of the inhabitants of the backward rural areas. (LCW 19.532.)

He observes that, if the principle of cultural-national autonomy had been applied in St. Petersburg, there would have been no less than twenty-three 'national associations', each with its own schools. He continues :

The interests of democracy in general and of the working class in particular demand the very opposite. We must strive to secure the *mixing* of the children of *all* nationalities in *uniform* schools in each locality. . . . It is not our business to segregate the nations in matters of education in any way; on the contrary, we must strive to create the fundamental democratic conditions for the peaceful coexistence of nations on the basis of equal rights. (LCW 19.532.)

Here, too, the solution lies in the fullest extension of democracy. Lenin shows this by taking an extreme case. After noting that the school population of St. Petersburg included one Georgian child, he remarks :

We may be asked whether it is possible to safeguard the interests of the *one* Georgian child among the 48,076 schoolchildren of St. Petersburg on the basis of equal rights. And we should reply that it is impossible to establish a special Georgian school in St. Petersburg on the basis of Georgian 'national culture'. . . . But we shall not be defending anything harmful, or striving after anything impossible, if we demand for this child free government premises for

66

lectures on the Georgian language, Georgian history, etc., the provision of Georgian books from the Central Library for this child, a state contribution towards the fees of the Georgian teacher, and so forth. Under real democracy ... the people can achieve this quite easily. But this real democracy can be achieved only when the workers of all nationalities are united. (LCW 19.533.)

5. *National and International Culture*

The bourgeoisie has always had a dual character, revolutionary in relation to the past, counter-revolutionary in relation to the future, and in the final stage of capitalism the negative aspect predominates. The class which once led the fight for national independence now imposes its rule on other nations. The culture which was once full of life and vigour now becomes a dead weight crushing the aspirations of subject peoples. In some cases the people itself is physically exterminated, like the American Indians and the Australian aborigines. In other cases the people is enslaved and its culture stamped out, like the South African Bantus. Elsewhere more subtle methods are employed :

The imperialists have never slackened their efforts to poison the minds of the Chinese people. This is their policy of cultural aggression. And it is carried out through missionary work, through establishing hospitals and schools, publishing newspapers, and inducing Chinese students to study abroad. Their aim is to train intellectuals who will serve their interests and to dupe the people. (MSW 2.312.)

The same dualism is revealed in the bourgeoisie of the oppressed nation, which wavers between its desire for national independence and its fear of socialism, and

67

so is always ready, as in Greece and Ireland, to sell its cultural heritage :

> 'We', the proletariat, have seen dozens of times how the bourgeoisie *betrays* the interests of freedom, motherland, language and nation, when it is confronted by the revolutionary proletariat. (LCW 6.462, cf. 23.61.)

From this it follows that the future of world culture, which is the sum total of national cultures, is in the hands of the international proletariat. What will that future be? This question has been answered in general terms both by Lenin and by Mao Tse-tung :

> The *elements* of democratic and socialist culture are present, if only in rudimentary form, in *every* national culture, since in every nation there are labouring and exploited masses, whose conditions of life inevitably give rise to the ideology of democracy and socialism. But *every* nation also possesses a bourgeois culture (and most nations a reactionary and clerical culture as well) in the form, not merely of 'elements', but of the *dominant* culture. Therefore the general national culture *is* the culture of the landlords, clergy and bourgeoisie. . . .
> In advancing the slogan of 'the international culture of democracy and the world working-class movement', we take from *each* national culture *only* its democratic and socialist elements; we take them *only* and *absolutely* in opposition to the bourgeois culture and bourgeois nationalism of each nation. (LCW 20.24.)

> We have said that China's new culture at the present stage is an anti-imperialist, anti-feudal culture of the masses of the people under the leadership of the proletariat. Today, anything that is truly of the masses must necessarily be led by the proletariat.

68

Whatever is under the leadership of the bourgeoisie cannot possibly be of the masses. Naturally, the same applies to the new literature and art which are part of the new culture. We should take over the rich legacy and the good traditions in literature and art that have been handed down from past ages in China and foreign countries, but the aim must still be to serve the masses of the people. Nor do we refuse to utilise the literary and artistic forms of the past, but in our hands these old forms, remoulded and infused with new content, also become something revolutionary in the service of the people. (MSW 3.76.)

The proletarian culture of the future will be international in content, national in form. It will be international, and therefore homogeneous, in content, because it will express the socialist outlook common to the masses of the people of all nations. It will be national, and therefore varied, in form, because that outlook will be embodied concretely in forms determined by the language, customs and traditions of each nation. As Stalin explained :

Proletarian in content, national in form—such is the universal culture towards which socialism is proceeding. Proletarian culture does not abolish national culture, it gives it content. On the other hand, national culture does not abolish proletarian culture, it gives it form. The slogan of national culture was a bourgeois slogan so long as the bourgeoisie was in power and the consolidation of nations proceeded under the aegis of the bourgeois order. The slogan of national culture became a proletarian slogan when the proletariat came to power, and when the consolidation of nations began to proceed under the aegis of Soviet power. (SCW 7.140.)

Similarly, Mao Tse-tung has said :

For the Chinese Communists, who are part of the great Chinese nation, flesh of its flesh and blood of its blood, any talk about Marxism in isolation from China's characteristics is merely Marxism in the abstract, Marxism in a vacuum. Hence to apply Marxism concretely in China, so that its every manifestation has an indubitably Chinese character, that is, to apply Marxism in the light of China's specific characteristics, becomes a problem which it is urgent for the whole Party to understand and solve. Foreign stereotypes must be abolished, there must be less singing of empty, abstract tunes, and dogmatism must be laid to rest; they must be replaced by the fresh, lively Chinese style and spirit which the common people of China love. To separate internationalist content from national form is the practice of those who do not understand the first thing about internationalism. (MSW 2.209, cf. 381.)

Mao Tse-tung is speaking here of Party propaganda, but what he says applies equally to culture; and not only to Chinese culture, but to the culture of all nations, great and small, old and new, including those which, after being crushed by imperialism and brought to the verge of extinction, will be saved by socialism. Thus, proletarian culture will be richer than bourgeois culture and infinitely more varied.

CHAPTER V

Socialism in One Country

The proletariat have nothing to lose but their chains. They have the world to win. Working-men of all countries, unite !

—*Communist Manifesto*

1. *Marx's Theory of Permanent Revolution*

Lenin's contribution to Marxist theory was defined by Stalin as follows :

> Leninism is Marxism of the era of imperialism and of the proletarian revolution. To be more exact, Leninism is the theory and practice of the proletarian revolution in general, the theory and tactics of the dictatorship of the proletariat in particular. Marx and Engels pursued their activities in the pre-revolutionary period (we have the proletarian revolution in mind), when developed imperialism did not yet exist, in the period of the proletariat's preparation for revolution, in the period when the proletarian revolution was not yet an immediate practical inevitability. Lenin, however, the disciple of Marx and Engels, pursued his activities in the period of developed imperialism, in the period of the unfolding proletarian revolution, when the proletarian revolution had already triumphed in one country, had smashed bourgeois democracy and had ushered in the era of proletarian democracy, the era of the Soviets. (SCW 6.73.)

The era of imperialism, or monopoly capitalism, opened in the last years of the nineteenth century and culminated in the October Revolution of 1917. It coincided, therefore, with the period of Lenin's activities, which began in the nineties and ended a few years after the revolution which he led. The theoretical analysis of imperialism was his, and so too was the leadership of the October Revolution. In this chapter it will be shown how, starting from the perspective of world revolution which had been outlined by Marx and Engels on the basis of their activities in the era of industrial capitalism, Lenin worked out a new perspective corresponding to the conditions of the imperialist era, which Marx and Engels did not live to see :

Marx, in the era of *laissez-faire* capitalism, could not concretely know certain laws peculiar to the era of imperialism beforehand, because imperialism, the last stage of capitalism, had not yet emerged and the relevant practice was lacking; only Lenin and Stalin could undertake this task. (MSW 1.299.)

In 1847, in a draft which served as a basis for the *Communist Manifesto*, Engels raised the question whether it was possible that the proletarian revolution might take place in one country alone :

Can this revolution take place in one country alone? No. Large-scale industry has, by the very fact that it has created a world market, bound all the nations of the earth, and notably the civilised nations, so closely together, that each depends on what is happening in the others. Further, in all the civilised countries it has evened up social development to such an extent that in all of them the bourgeoisie and the proletariat have become the two decisive classes of society, and the struggle between them the major struggle of our times. Therefore, the communist revolution will not be simply a national revolution, but will take place simultaneously in all the civilised countries, that is, at least in England, America, France and Germany. (Quoted in SCW 8.260, cf. 7.237.)

In the final draft of the *Manifesto* the idea of 'simultaneous revolution' was not mentioned. The authors confined their attention to the situation in Germany, where the bourgeois revolution had not yet taken place :

The Communists turn their attention chiefly to Germany, because that country is on the eve of a bourgeois revolution that is bound to be carried out under more advanced conditions of European civilisation, and with a much more developed proletariat, than that of England in the seventeenth and of France in the eighteenth century, and because the bourgeois revolution in Germany will be but the prelude to an immediately following proletarian revolution. (ME 1.65.)

A full analysis of the situation in Germany, together with a forecast of the further perspective, was given by Marx in 1850 :

While the democratic petty bourgeoisie wish to bring the revolution to a conclusion as quickly as possible and with the achievement at most of the above demands, it is our interest and our task to make the revolution permanent, until all the more or less possessing classes have been displaced from domination, until the proletariat has conquered state power, and the association of proletarians, not only in one country but in all the dominant countries of the world, has advanced so far that competition among the proletarians of these countries has ceased

73

and that at least the decisive forces are concentrated in the hands of the proletarians. (ME 1.110.)

In this forecast the impending revolution is described as 'permanent'. It is to begin with a bourgeois revolution in Germany, which will be followed without interruption by a proletarian revolution in that country, and that in turn will be carried into the other advanced countries of the West, until the proletariat has established its supremacy all over the world; and meanwhile the transition from the lower stage of communism (that is, socialism) to the higher stage will have begun. This idea of 'permanent revolution'—that is, revolution continuing by stages—marks the central point at which the Marxist theory differs both from reformism (which eliminates the revolution) and from anarchism (which eliminates the stages).

Further, as Marx explained, the success of the revolution in Germany would depend on the skill with which the proletariat handled its relations with the peasantry. In the first stage, directed against the feudalists and their allies among the big bourgeoisie, the proletariat was to 'march together' with the democratic petty bourgeoisie (including the peasantry); in the second stage, it was to advance beyond the petty-bourgeois demands and initiate the proletarian revolution. Analysing the reasons for the defeat of the German revolution, Engels pointed to the failure of the proletariat to establish close ties with the peasantry :

The mass of the nation, small bourgeois artisans and peasants, were left in the lurch by their nearest and natural allies, the bourgeoisie, because they were too revolutionary, and partly also by the proletariat, because they were not sufficiently advanced. (MEP 152.)

After the Peasant Reform of 1861 Marx and Engels

looked to Russia as 'the vanguard of revolutionary action in Europe' and envisaged the possibility that a bourgeois revolution in that country might become 'the signal for a proletarian revolution in the West' (ME 1.24, cf. 2.60). In other words, Russia might play the part which they had previously assigned to Germany. They still believed that, when the proletarian revolution did come, it would be simultaneous.

Lastly, the proletarian revolution was to issue in the dictatorship of the proletariat. This concept is already implicit in the *Manifesto* (in the sentence quoted at the head of Chapter I) but was first expressly formulated by Marx in 1852 :

> And now, as to myself, no credit is due to me for discovering the existence of classes in modern society or the struggle between them. Long before me bourgeois historians had described the historical development of this class struggle and bourgeois economists the economic anatomy of classes. What I did that was new was to prove : (1) that the *existence of classes* is only bound up with *particular historical phases in the development of production;* (2) that the class struggle necessarily leads to the *dictatorship of the proletariat*; (3) that this dictatorship itself only constitutes the transition to the *abolition of all classes* and to a *classless society.* (ME 2.452.)

One essential element in the concept was still lacking— the need for the proletariat to destroy the bourgeois state machine. This was one of the lessons of the Paris Commune, as Engels explained :

> The Commune was compelled to recognise from the outset that the working class, once come to power, could not carry on business with the old state machine; that in order not to lose again its newly-won supremacy, it must, on the one hand, do away

with all the old repressive machinery previously used against it, and, on the other, safeguard itself against its own deputies and officials by declaring them all without exception subject to recall at any moment. (ME 1.483.)

In these ideas of Marx and Engels we recognise the three main features of Lenin's revolutionary strategy as described above in Chapters I-III · the dictatorship of the proletariat, the uninterrupted transition from the bourgeois to the proletarian revolution, and the worker-peasant alliance. There is, however, one point at which Lenin's perspective, in the form which it eventually assumed on the eve of the October Revolution, differed sharply from theirs.

2. *The Victory of the October Revolution*

As we have seen, Marx and Engels believed that the proletarian revolution would break out simultaneously in the advanced countries of the West, sparked off perhaps by a bourgeois revolution in Russia. From this it followed by implication that, if it should be attempted (as in the Paris Commune) in a single country without the support of similar revolutions elsewhere, it would be unable to survive.

For many years Lenin accepted these assumptions :

We will make the Russian political revolution the prelude to the socialist revolution in Europe. (LCW 8.303, cf 541, 9.57, 412, 433.)

The Russian revolution can achieve victory by its own efforts, but it cannot possibly hold and consolidate its gains by its own strength alone. It cannot do this unless there is a socialist revolution in the West. (LCW 10.280, cf. 92, 334, 394, 13.327.)

Lenin never ceased to believe that 'the objective conditions in Western Europe were ripe for a socialist revolution' (LCW 21.419); but, after the collapse of the Second International in 1914, when the working-class leaders of the West repudiated their pledges to oppose the imperialist war, he recognised that the subjective conditions had become unfavourable :

In the early period of the revolution many entertained the hope that the socialist revolution would begin in Western Europe immediately the imperialist war ended. At the time when the masses were armed there could have been a successful revolution in some of the Western countries as well. It could have taken place but for the fact that the split within the proletariat of Western Europe was deeper, and the treachery of the former socialist leaders greater, than had been imagined. (LCW 30.417, cf. 32.481.)

Meanwhile, in the course of his work on imperialism he had reached the conclusion that, in the new world situation, the old theory of 'simultaneous' revolution, which implied that a proletarian revolution attempted in a single country could not be successful, was out of date :

Uneven economic and political development is an absolute law of capitalism. Hence, the victory of socialism is possible first in several or even in one capitalist country taken separately. The victorious proletariat of that country, having expropriated the capitalists and organised socialist production, would stand up against the rest of the world, the capitalist world, attracting to its cause the oppressed classes of other countries, raising revolts in those countries against the capitalists, and in the event of necessity coming out even with armed force against the exploiting classes and their states. (LCW 21.342.)

In 1916 he went further, asserting that the socialist revolution *could* not be simultaneous :

The development of capitalism proceeds extremely unevenly in different countries. It cannot be otherwise under commodity production. From this it follows irrefutably that socialism cannot achieve victory simultaneously in *all* countries. It will achieve victory first in one or several, while the others will remain for some time bourgeois or pre-bourgeois. (LCW 23.79.)

And, after the new socialist republic had emerged victorious from the war of intervention and the civil war, he declared :

It has turned out that, while our forecasts did not materialise simply, rapidly and directly, they were fulfilled in so far as we achieved the main thing. The possibility has been maintained of the existence of proletarian rule and the Soviet Republic even in the event of the world socialist revolution being delayed. (LCW 31.411.)

But is the existence of a socialist republic in a capitalist environment at all conceivable? From the political and military aspects it seemed inconceivable. That it *is* possible, both politically and militarily, has now been proved. It is a fact. (LCW 33.151.)

In reaching this conclusion, Lenin did not mean to imply that the survival of the Soviet republic was thenceforth guaranteed. On the contrary, he continued to maintain that the victory of socialism could not be regarded as final until it had been won on a world scale :

The final victory of socialism in a single country is of course impossible. (LCW 26.470.)

Everyone knows the difficulties of a revolution. It may begin with brilliant success in one country and then go through agonising periods, since final victory is only possible on a world scale, and only by the joint efforts of the workers of all countries. (LCW 27.372.)

We have always known, and shall never forget, that ours is an international cause, and that, until the revolution takes place in all lands, including the richest and most highly civilised, our victory will be only a half-victory, perhaps even less. (LCW 31.399.)

We have always said that we are only a single link in the chain of world revolution. (LCW 31.431, cf. 32.361.)

3. *Uneven Development*

In rejecting the theory of simultaneous revolution Lenin appealed to the law of the uneven development of capitalist society.

Uneven development, arising as it does from the nature of commodity production, is found in all stages of capitalist society, and indeed also in pre-capitalist society, in so far as it too reveals rudimentary forms of commodity production; but, just as capitalism marks the highest stage in the growth of commodity production, the stage at which labour-power becomes a commodity, so it is in the era of imperialism, the highest stage of capitalism, that the law of uneven development becomes a major factor in world revolution. All this was shown by Lenin in his study of imperialism. His argument may be presented in the form in which it was later summarised by Stalin in dealing with the question at issue :

What is the law of the uneven development of capitalism, whose operation under the conditions of imperialism leads to the victory of socialism in one country?

Speaking of this law, Lenin held that the old, pre-monopoly capitalism had already passed into imperialism; that the world economy is developing in the conditions of a frenzied struggle between the leading imperialist groups for territory, markets, raw materials, etc.; that the division of the world into spheres of influence between the imperialist groups is already complete; that the development of capitalist countries does not proceed evenly, not in such a way that one country follows after another or advances parallel with it, but spasmodically, through some countries which had previously outstripped the others being pushed back and new countries advancing to the forefront; that this manner of development in the capitalist countries inevitably engenders conflicts and wars between the capitalist powers for a fresh redivision of an already divided world; that these conflicts and wars lead to the weakening of imperialism; that owing to this the world imperialist front becomes easily liable to be breached in individual countries; and that because of this the victory of socialism in individual countries becomes possible.

We know that quite recently Britain was ahead of all the other imperialist states. We also know that Germany then began to overtake Britain and demanded a 'place in the sun' at the expense of other countries and in the first place of Britain. We know that it was precisely as a result of this circumstance that the imperialist war of 1914-18 arose. Now, after the imperialist war, America has spurted far ahead and out-distanced both Britain and the other European powers. It can scarcely be doubted that this contains the seeds of great new conflicts and wars.

The fact that in consequence of the imperialist war the imperialist front was breached in Russia is evidence that in the present-day conditions of capitalist development the chain of the imperialist front will not necessarily break in the country where industry is most developed, but where the chain is weakest, where the proletariat has an important ally—such as the peasantry, for instance—in the fight against imperialist rule, as was the case in Russia. (SCW 8.265.)

In Russia, the law of uneven development operated in such a way as to turn the balance of class forces in favour of the proletariat :

Owing to a number of historical causes—the greater backwardness of Russia, the unusual hardships inflicted on her by the war, the utter rottenness of Tsarism, and the extreme tenacity of the traditions of 1905—the revolution broke out earlier in Russia than in other countries. (LCW 25.364, cf. 29.307.)

In the West, however, where the bourgeoisie was firmly established and the proletariat divided, the first step in the revolution—the seizure of state power—was bound to be more difficult :

It would be a very great illusion, a very great mistake, to forget that it was easy for the Russian revolution to begin but difficult for it to take further steps. This was inevitable, because we had to begin with the most backward and rotten political system. The European revolution will have to begin against the bourgeoisie, a much more serious enemy, and under immeasurably more difficult conditions. (LCW 27.176, cf. 98.)

Thus, the effect of imperialism was to speed up the revolution in the backward country and slow it down in the more advanced. Such are the dialectics of uneven development.

4. Revolution in the East

After the October Revolution it became clear that the next advance of the world revolution would not necessarily be confined to Europe. The imperialists had succeeded for the time being in containing the revolution in the West, but they could not prevent the victory of the October Revolution from reverberating like thunder all round the world :

> I think that what the Red Army has accomplished—its struggle and the history of its victory—will be of colossal, epoch-making significance for all the peoples of the East. It will show them that, weak as they may be, invincible as may seem the power of their European oppressors, who in the struggle employ all the marvels of technology and military art—even so, a revolutionary war waged by oppressed peoples, if it really succeeds in arousing the workers and the exploited in their millions, harbours such potentialities, such miracles, that the emancipation of the peoples of the East is now quite practicable, from the standpoint not only of the prospects of the international revolution, but also of the direct military experience acquired in Asia, in Siberia—the experience of the Soviet republic, which has suffered armed invasion from all the powerful imperialist countries. (LCW 30.153.)

Hence, there was now being forged in the East, where conditions were even more backward than they had been in Russia, a new link in the chain of world revolution :

> Meanwhile, India and China are seething. They represent over 700 million people, and together with the neighbouring Asian countries, which are in all ways similar to them, over half the world's inhabitants. Inexorably and with mounting momentum

they are approaching their 1905, with the essential and important difference that in 1905 the revolution in Russia could still (at any rate in the beginning) proceed in isolation, that is, without other countries being immediately drawn in; whereas the revolutions now maturing in India and China are being—have already been—drawn into the revolutionary struggle, the revolutionary movement, the world revolution. (LCW 33.350.)

The impact of the October Revolution in China has been described by Mao Tse-tung :

It was through the Russians that the Chinese found Marxism. Before the October Revolution, the Chinese were not only ignorant of Lenin and Stalin, they did not even know of Marx and Engels. The salvoes of the October Revolution brought us Marxism-Leninism. The October Revolution helped progressives in China, as throughout the world, to adopt the proletarian world outlook as the instrument for studying a nation's destiny and considering anew their old problems. Follow the path of the Russians—that was their conclusion. (MSW 4.413.)

Ten years later, when the first wave of the Chinese revolution had expended itself, ending in defeat for the revolutionary forces, many comrades, misled by the outward appearance of things, despaired of China's future. In this situation Mao Tse-tung wrote :

Although the subjective forces of the revolution in China are now weak, so also are all organisations (organs of political power, armed forces, political parties, etc.) of the reactionary ruling classes, resting as they do on the backward and fragile social and economic structure of China. This helps to explain why revolution cannot break out at once in the countries of Western Europe, where, although the subjective forces of revolution are now perhaps somewhat stronger than in China, the forces of the reactionary ruling classes are many times stronger, and it also helps to explain why the revolution will undoubtedly move towards a high tide more rapidly in China, for although the subjective forces of the revolution in China at present are weak, the forces of the counter-revolution are relatively weak too. (MSW 1.119.)

By 'the subjective forces of the revolution' are meant the organised forces of the revolution. These forces, it is argued here, were really, despite appearances, stronger in China than in the West, because the forces ranged against them were weaker. Further, the situation in China was such that the revolutionary forces were bound to grow :

In other words, our forces, though small at present, will grow very rapidly. In the conditions prevailing in China, their growth is not only possible but indeed inevitable, as the May 30th movement and the Great Revolution which followed have fully proved. When we look at a thing, we must examine its essence and treat its appearance merely as an usher at the threshold, and once we cross the threshold, we must grasp the essence of the thing; this is the only reliable and scientific method of analysis. (MSW 1.119.)

Turning to India, we find there a broadly similar set of conditions, but the balance of forces was different. On the one hand, in British India capitalist relations were more highly developed, and the big bourgeoisie was more united, being tied to a single imperialist power, not torn between rival powers, as in China (MSW 2.443). At the same time, feudal relations still survived, especially in the native states. On the other hand, the proletariat failed to establish an alliance with the peasantry. Thus, the counter-revolutionary forces were stronger and the revolutionary forces weaker than in China. The result was that the bourgeoisie retained the leadership of the national movement and came to terms with feudalism and imperialism.

In the summer of 1945, when the war in the West was at an end and the surrender of Japan already assured, the American imperialists used their latest technological marvel to wipe out two Japanese cities. The purpose of this action, which must be counted as one of the greatest crimes in the whole history of warfare, was to intimidate all those, especially in Russia and China, who might dare to challenge the world's new masters. At the same time they were pouring money and war materials into the rotten regime of Chiang Kai-shek in the hope that he would destroy communism in China, which they would then use as a base for a renewed war against the Soviet Union. Four years later Chiang Kai-shek was routed by workers and peasants trained in Mao Tse-tung's strategy of people's war (which was derived partly from the experience of the Red Army in the Russian civil war); and a people's democratic dictatorship was established in Peking. Imperialism had suffered a second shattering blow.

CHAPTER VI

The Party

> The Communists fight for the attainment of the immediate aims, for the enforcement of the momentary interests, of the working class; but in the movement of the present they also represent and take care of the future of that movement.
>
> —*Communist Manifesto*

1. *Lessons of the Paris Commune*

On March 18, 1871, when the French bourgeoisie had capitulated to the Prussian invaders rather than fight on with working-class support, the workers of Paris revolted and seized power. In place of the bourgeois parliament they set up the Commune, which had executive as well as legislative functions. Its members were elected by universal suffrage and subject to instant recall. The standing army was abolished and replaced by the armed people; the police were brought directly under popular control; the magistrates and all other public officials were elected by the workers and paid a workman's wages. This was the first time in history that the proletariat had succeeded in overthrowing the bourgeoisie and setting up its own state; and, although the Communards were not Marxists, the new state assumed in their hands the form of a proletarian dictatorship as conceived by Marx and Engels. Engels wrote later:

> Well and good, gentlemen; do you want to know

what this dictatorship looks like? Look at the Paris Commune. That was the dictatorship of the proletariat. (ME 1.485.)

The Commune lasted only a few weeks. There was no working-class party, the trade-union movement was still in its infancy, and through lack of experience the leaders made some serious mistakes. They were too lenient to the enemy, and they did not succeed in establishing a worker-peasant alliance. Above all, being preoccupied with armed struggle against the troops encircling the city, they had little time for socialist construction (LCW 17.141). At the end of May the Commune was overthrown, and the workers of Paris—men, women, children—were massacred in thousands by the riflemen of that same bourgeoisie which only eighty years before had overthrown the feudal monarchy in the name of liberty, equality and fraternity.

And yet, regarded historically, it was not a failure. Referring to Marx's judgement of it, Lenin wrote :

> In September 1870 Marx had called the insurrection an act of desperate folly; but in April 1871, when he saw the mass movement of the people, he watched it with the keen attention of a participant in great events marking a step forward in the historic revolutionary movement. (LCW 12.109.)

Not only was it the first proletarian dictatorship, but its organisational unit, the commune, was the prototype of the Soviets of Workers' Deputies, which sprang up in Russia in 1905 and again in 1917 :

> Only the Soviet organisation of the state can really effect the immediate break-up and total destruction of the old—that is, bourgeois—bureaucratic and judicial machinery, which has been—and inevitably had to be—retained even in

the most democratic republics, and which is, in actual fact, the greatest obstacle to the practical implementation of democracy for the workers and working-people generally. The Paris Commune took the first epoch-making step along this path. The Soviet system has taken the second. (LCW 28.466.)

The lessons to be learnt from the experience of 1871 were embodied by Lenin in the work of the revolutionary party which he founded and led; and of those lessons one of the most important was precisely the need for such a party—a party equipped with a revolutionary theory, united within itself by a combination of democracy and discipline, and bound by close ties to the masses.

2. *The Party of a New Type*

The theoretical principles underlying the organisation of a proletarian party were worked out by Lenin in the period which began with the preparations for the revolution of 1905 and ended with the October Revolution. During the greater part of this period the Party was banned, with only brief intervals of legality, and it was subject throughout to persecution from the Tsarist police. In these circumstances it was necessary that the leadership should consist of a solid core of professional revolutionaries :

I assert : (1) that no revolutionary movement can endure without a stable organisation of leaders maintaining continuity; (2) that the broader the popular mass drawn spontaneously into the struggle, forming the basis of the movement and participating in it, the greater the need for such an organisation and the more solid it must be ...; (3) that the organisation must consist chiefly of people professionally engaged in revolutionary activity; (4) that in an autocratic state, the more we *confine* membership of such an organisation to professional revolutionaries trained in the art of combating the political police, the more difficult it will be to unearth the organisation and (5) the greater the number of people from the working class and other social classes who will be able to join the movement and work actively in it. (LCW 5.464.)

The need for a highly centralised leadership was driven home by the following experience :

The rapid alternation of legal and illegal work, which made it necessary to keep the general staff— the leaders—under cover and cloak them in the greatest secrecy, sometimes gave rise to extremely dangerous consequences. The worst of these was that in 1912 the *agent provocateur* Malinovsky got into the Bolshevik Central Committee. He betrayed scores and scores of the best and most loyal comrades, caused them to be sent to penal servitude, and hastened the death of many of them. (LCW 31.45.)

At the same time, if the members of the Party were to work together effectively, it was necessary that they should act on the basis of collective decisions reached after full and free discussion. This principle of unity in action combined with freedom of criticism is the basis of democratic centralism.

When the Party emerged above ground in 1917, it contained a core of trained revolutionaries, but at that time there was a large influx of new members, who did not recognise the need for Party discipline. Among these was Trotsky, who joined in July 1917. Lenin's principles were upheld by Stalin, who succeeded in the face of bitter opposition in establishing a collective leadership, but despite repeated efforts, extended over many years (SCW 6.238, 7.20, 31, 161, 10.328, 11.75, 137, 12.322), he was unable to check the growth of bureaucracy and came to rely himself increasingly on administrative methods, with the result that the relationship between the Party and the masses was impaired.

Meanwhile Lenin's principles were being applied in China by Mao Tse-tung. There, too, the Party had suffered savage persecution (MSW 2.376); but, thanks to the vast extent of the country, offering ample room for manoeuvre in a peasant war, the Communists were able to establish liberated areas, some of which they administered for many years before 1949. In this way they accumulated a fund of practical experience, which, combined with a close study of the history of the Bolshevik Party, enabled them to carry the theory and practice of democratic centralism forward to a higher stage.

Lenin's theory of the 'party of a new type', as developed by Mao Tse-tung, may be considered under three heads: the vanguard Party; democratic centralism; and the mass line.

3. *The Vanguard Party*

The proletariat, as it becomes conscious of its role in history, organises itself as the vanguard of the other exploited classes, principally the petty bourgeoisie, giving them leadership, winning their support, and at the same time opposing the vacillations and deviations which they bring with them into the movement. This it can only do if it is itself organised under the leadership of an independent proletarian party:

In its struggle for power the proletariat has no other weapon but organisation. Disunited by the rule of anarchical competition in the bourgeois world, ground down by forced labour for capital, constantly thrust back into the 'lower depths' of utter destitution, savagery and degeneration, the proletariat can become—and will inevitably become—an invincible force only when its ideological unification in accordance with the principles of Marxism is consolidated by the material unity of organisation, which welds millions of toilers into an army of the working class. (LCW 7.415.)

A Social-Democrat must never for a moment forget that the proletariat will inevitably have to wage a class struggle for socialism even against the most democratic and republican bourgeoisie and petty bourgeoisie. That is beyond doubt. Hence the absolute necessity of a separate, independent, strictly class Party of Social-Democracy. (LCW 9.85.)

The Party is the politically conscious, advanced section of the class. It is its vanguard. The strength of that vanguard is a hundred times, more than a hundred times, greater than its numbers. (LCW 19.406.)

One of the greatest and most dangerous mistakes made by Communists (as generally by revolutionaries who have successfully accomplished the beginning of a great revolution) is the idea that a revolution can be made by revolutionaries alone. On the contrary, if it is to be successful, all serious revolutionary work requires that we should understand and translate into action the idea that revolutionaries can only play the part of vanguard of the truly virile and advanced class. A vanguard performs its task as vanguard only when it is able to avoid isolation from the people it leads and is really able to lead the whole mass forward. (LCW 33.227.)

In order to carry out its task as vanguard, the Party must learn to handle correctly the relations between the proletariat and the several sections of the petty bourgeoisie and the relations between different sections of the proletariat itself :

Capitalism would not be capitalism if the proletariat *pur sang* were not surrounded by some very motley types, intermediate between the proletarian and the semi-proletarian (who earns his livelihood in part by selling his labour-power), between the semi-proletarian and the small peasant (and petty artisan, handicraft-worker, and small master in general), between the small peasant and the middle peasant, and so on, and if the proletariat itself were not divided into more or less developed strata, if it were not divided according to territorial origin, trade, sometimes according to religion, and so on. From all this follows the necessity, the absolute necessity, for the Communist Party, the vanguard of the proletariat, its class-conscious section, to resort to changes of tack, to conciliation and compromises with the various groups of proletarians, with the various parties of the workers and small masters. It is entirely a matter of *knowing how* to apply these tactics in such a way as to raise, not lower, the *general* level of proletarian class-consciousness, of revolutionary spirit, of the ability to fight and win. (LCW 31.74.)

The Chinese Party was faced with similar problems in establishing its alliance with the petty bourgeoisie :

Among the petty-bourgeois masses outside the

Party, in addition to the peasants who form the main force in the Chinese bourgeois-democratic revolution, the urban petty bourgeoisie is also one of the motive forces of the revolution in the present stage, because the great majority of its members are subject to all kinds of oppression, are being constantly and rapidly driven to poverty, bankruptcy and unemployment, and very urgently demand economic and political democracy. But, as a class in transition, the petty bourgeoisie has a dual character. As for its good and revolutionary side, the great majority of this class are receptive to the political and organisational influence of the proletariat, and even to its ideological influence, at present they demand a democratic revolution and are capable of uniting and fighting for it, and in the future they can take the path of socialism together with the proletariat; but as for its bad and backward side, not only has this class various weaknesses which distinguish it from the proletariat, but when deprived of proletarian leadership, it often veers and falls under the influence of the liberal bourgeoisie, and becomes their prisoner. In the present stage, therefore, the proletariat and its vanguard, the Communist Party of China, should base themselves on a firm and broad alliance with the masses of the petty bourgeoisie outside the Party, and should, on the one hand, be lenient in dealing with them and tolerate their liberal ideas and style of work, in so far as these do not impede the struggle against the enemy or disrupt the social life we share in common, and, on the other, give them appropriate education so as to strengthen our alliance with them. (MSW 3.214.)

4. Democratic Centralism

Party discipline rests on democracy under centralised leadership. In this way freedom of discussion and criticism is combined with unity in action. The lower bodies elect the higher and are subject to their control. Majority decisions are binding. These principles correspond to every class-conscious worker's experience of trade-union struggle :

> We have already more than once enunciated our theoretical views on the importance of discipline and how this concept is to be understood in the party of the working class. We defined it as *unity of action, freedom of discussion and criticism.* Only such discipline is worthy of the democratic party of the advanced class. The strength of the working class lies in organisation. Unless the masses are organised, the proletariat is nothing. Organised—it is everything. Organisation means unity of action, unity in practical operations. . . . Therefore the proletariat does not recognise unity of action without freedom to discuss and criticise. (LCW 11.320.)

> Is it really so difficult to understand that, *before* a decision has been taken by the centre on a strike, it is permissible to agitate for and against it, but that *after* a decision in favour of a strike (with the additional decision to conceal this from the enemy) to carry on agitation against the strike is strike-breaking? Any worker will understand that. (LCW 26.224.)

When the Party is working illegally, the scope for discussion and criticism is necessarily restricted, but at the same time there can be no discipline without confidence in the leadership. The terms of admission to the Third (Communist) International, founded in 1920, included the following :

94

Parties belonging to the Communist International must be organised on the principle of democratic *centralism*. In this period of acute civil war, the Communist Parties can perform their duty only if they are organised in a most centralised manner, are marked by an iron discipline bordering on military discipline, and have strong, authoritative party centres invested with wide powers and enjoying the unanimous confidence of the membership. (LCW 31.210.)

In the course of a long struggle to build the Bolshevik Party on this basis, Lenin had to combat the anarchistic attitude to discipline prevalent among the Menshevik intellectuals. To one of these, who complained that he looked on the Party as though it were 'a huge factory', Lenin replied :

This dreadful word of his at once betrays the mentality of the bourgeois intellectual unfamiliar with either the practice or the theory of proletarian organisation. For the factory, which to some seems only a bogey, represents that highest form of capitalist co-operation which has united and disciplined the proletariat, taught it to organise, and placed it at the head of all the other sections of the toiling and exploited population. And Marxism, which is the ideology of the proletariat trained by capitalism, has been, and is, training unstable intellectuals to distinguish between the factory as a means of exploitation (discipline based on fear of starvation) and the factory as a means of organisation (discipline based on collective labour united by the conditions of a technically advanced form of production). The discipline and organisation which come so hard to the bourgeois intellectual are easily acquired by the proletariat just because of this factory 'schooling'. (LCW 7.391.)

This is where the proletarian who has been through the school of the 'factory' can and should teach a lesson to anarchistic individualism. The class-conscious worker has long since emerged from the state of infancy when he used to fight shy of the intellectual as such. The class-conscious worker appreciates the richer store of knowledge and the wider political outlook which he finds among Social-Democratic intellectuals. But, as we proceed with the building of a *real* Party, the class-conscious worker must learn to distinguish the mentality of the soldier of the proletarian army from the mentality of the bourgeois intellectual who parades anarchistic phrases; he must learn to *insist* that the duties of the Party member be fulfilled not only by the rank and file but by the 'people at the top' as well. (LCW 7.394.)

The circumstances in which the Chinese Party was built were different, and in some respects less difficult, since the Bolsheviks had blazed the trail; but the principles at issue were the same :

If we are to make the Party strong, we must practise democratic centralism to stimulate the initiative of the whole membership. There was more centralism during the period of reaction and civil war. In the new period, centralism must be closely linked with democracy. Let us apply democracy, and so give scope to initiative throughout the Party. Let us give scope to the initiative of the whole Party membership, and so train new cadres in great numbers, eliminate the remnants of sectarianism, and unite the whole Party as solidly as steel. (MSW 1.292.)

For these reasons, education in democracy must be carried on within the Party so that members can understand the meaning of democratic life, the meaning of the relationship between democracy and centralism, and the way in which democratic centralism should be put into practice. Only in this way can we really extend democracy within the Party and at the same time avoid ultra-democracy and the *laissez-faire* which destroys discipline. (MSW 2.205.)

The Chinese Party attracted recruits in large numbers, not only from the peasantry, but from the urban petty bourgeoisie and particularly the intellectuals; but these, too, became good Party members only after submitting to a process of ideological remoulding in accordance with the principles formulated by Lenin :

But the case is entirely different with those of petty-bourgeois origin who have voluntarily abandoned their original class stand and joined the party of the proletariat. The Party should adopt a policy towards them that differs in principle from that towards the petty-bourgeois masses outside the Party. Since such people were close to the proletariat to begin with and joined its Party voluntarily, they can gradually become proletarian in their ideology through Marxist-Leninist education in the Party and steeling in mass revolutionary struggles, and they can be of great service to the proletarian forces. . . . It has to be emphasised, however, that the revolutionary character of the petty bourgeois who has not yet been proletarianised is essentially different from the revolutionary character of the proletarian, and that this difference can often develop into a state of antagonism. . . . If the advanced elements of the proletariat do not draw a firm and sharp line between Marxist-Leninist ideology and the original ideology of those Party members who came from the petty bourgeoisie, and do not educate them and struggle with them in a serious but appropriate and patient way, it will be impossible to overcome their petty-bourgeois ideology, and, what is more, these members will inevitably strive to remould the vanguard of the proletariat in their own image and usurp Party leadership, thus damaging the cause of the Party and the people. (MSW 3.214.)

In the Chinese democratic revolutionary movement, it was the intellectuals who were first to awaken. . . . But the intellectuals will accomplish nothing if they fail to integrate themselves with the workers and peasants. In the final analysis. the dividing line between revolutionary intellectuals and non-revolutionary or counter-revolutionary intellectuals is whether or not they are willing to integrate themselves with the workers and peasants and actually do so. (MSW 2.238.)

Lastly, democratic centralism is the organising principle, not only of the proletarian party, but of the new proletarian state, based in Russia on the soviets and in China on the people's congresses :

Now, if the proletariat and poor peasants take state power into their own hands, organise themselves quite freely in communes, and *unite* the action of all the communes in striking at capital, in crushing the resistance of the capitalists, and transferring the privately-owned railways, factories, land and so on to the *entire* nation, to the whole of society, won't that be centralism? Won't that be the most consistent democratic centralism and moreover proletarian centralism? (LCW 25.429.)

The organisational principle of the new-democratic state should be democratic centralism, with the people's congresses determining the major policies and electing the governments at the various levels. It is at once democratic and centralised, that is, centralised on the basis of democracy and democratic under centralised guidance. This is the only system that can give full expression to democracy with full powers vested in the people's congresses at all levels and, at the same time, guarantee centralised administration with the governments at each level exercising centralised management of all the affairs entrusted to them by the people's congresses at the corresponding level and safeguarding whatever is essential to the democratic life of the people. (MSW 3,280, cf. 2.57, 352, MFE 86.)

5. *From the Masses, to the Masses*

One of the fundamental principles of Party work, as developed in China, is what is known as 'the mass line', that is, the systematic cultivation of the closest possible interaction between the Party and the masses. This was one of the lessons which the Chinese Party learnt from the Russian Revolution :

The more acute the class struggle becomes, the more necessary it is for the proletariat to rely, most resolutely and completely, on the broad masses of the people and to bring into full play their revolutionary enthusiasm to defeat the counter-revolutionary forces. The experience of the stirring and seething mass struggles in the Soviet Union during the October Revolution and the ensuing civil war proved this truth to the full. It is from Soviet experience in that period that the 'mass line' our Party so often talks about was derived. (HE 20.)

If the party is to lead the masses, it must serve

their interests. It must serve in order to lead. It must, therefore, be in close contact with them. Only in this way can it guide their activities and correct its own mistakes :

> To serve the masses and express *their* interests, having correctly conceived those interests, the advanced contingent, the organisation, must carry on all its activities among the masses, drawing from them all the best elements without exception, at every step verifying carefully and objectively whether contact with the masses is being maintained and whether it is a live contact. In this way, and only in this way, does the advanced contingent train and enlighten the masses, expressing *their* interests, teaching them organisation and directing *all* their activities along the path of conscious class politics. (LCW 19.409.)

> A political party's attitude to its own mistakes is one of the most important and surest ways of judging how earnest the party is and how it fulfils in practice its obligations to its *class* and the *working people*. Frankly acknowledging a mistake, analysing the conditions that have led up to it, and thrashing out the means of rectifying it—that is the hallmark of a serious party; that is how it should perform its duties; that is how it should educate and train its *class* and then the *masses*. (LCW 31.57.)

This principle of 'the mass line' is regarded as the starting-point of all work in the Chinese Party :

> All work done for the masses must start from their needs and not from the desire of any individual, however well-intentioned. It often happens that objectively the masses need a certain change, but subjectively they are not as yet conscious of the

need, not yet willing or determined to make the change. In such cases we should wait patiently. We should not make the change until, through our work, most of the masses have become conscious of the need and are willing and determined to carry it out. Otherwise we shall isolate ourselves from the masses. (MSW 3.236.)

Our point of departure is to serve the people whole-heartedly and never for a moment divorce ourselves from the masses, to proceed in all cases from the interests of the people and not from the interests of individuals or groups, and to understand the identity of our responsibility to the people and our responsibility to the leading organs of the Party. Communists must be ready at all times to stand up for the truth, because truth is in the interests of the people; Communists must be ready at all times to correct their mistakes, because mistakes are against the interests of the people. Twenty-four years of experience tell us that the right task, policy and style of work invariably conform to the demands of the masses at a given time and place and invariably strengthen our ties with the masses, and the wrong task, policy and style of work invariably disagree with the demands of the masses at a given time and place and invariably alienate us from the masses. (MSW 3.315.)

We Communists are like seeds and the people are like the soil. Wherever we go, we must unite with the people, take root and blossom among them. Wherever our comrades go, they must build good relations with the masses, be concerned for them and help them to overcome their difficulties. We must unite with the masses; the more of the masses we unite with, the better. We must go all out to mobilise the masses, expand the people's forces, and, under the leadership of our Party, defeat the aggressor and build a new China. (MSW 4.58.)

We must criticise and struggle with certain cadres and Party members, who have committed serious mistakes, and certain bad elements among the masses of workers and peasants. In such criticism and struggle we should persuade the masses to adopt correct methods and forms and to refrain from rough actions. This is one side of the matter. The other side is that these cadres, Party members and bad elements should be made to pledge that they will not retaliate against the masses. It should be announced that the masses not only have the right to criticise them freely but also have the right to dismiss them from their posts when necessary, or to propose their dismissal, or to propose their expulsion from the Party and even to hand the worst elements over to the people's courts for trial and punishment. (MSW 4.186.)

The relation between the Party and the masses, like the relation between the Party leadership and the rank-and-file, is a unity of opposites, in which each acts and reacts upon the other :

As Comrade Mao Tse-tung says, the correct political line should be 'from the masses, to the masses'. To ensure that the line really comes from the masses, and in particular that it really goes back to the masses, there must be close ties not only between the Party and the masses outside the Party (between the class and the people) but above all between the Party's leading bodies and the masses within the Party (between the cadres and the rank-and-file); in other words, there must be a correct organisational line. (MSW 3.208.)

Further, this cyclical interaction between Party and

people corresponds to the dialectical relation between theory and practice in the Marxist theory of knowledge:

In all the practical work of our Party, all correct leadership is necessarily 'from the masses, to the masses'. This means: take the ideas of the masses (scattered and unsystematic ideas) and concentrate them (through study turn them into concentrated and systematic ideas), then go back to the masses and propagate and explain these ideas, until the masses embrace them as their own, hold fast to them and translate them into action, and test the correctness of these ideas in such action. Then once again concentrate ideas from the masses and once again go to the masses, so that the ideas are persevered in and carried through. And so on over and over again in an endless spiral, with the ideas becoming more correct, more vital and richer each time. Such is the Marxist theory of knowledge. (MSW 3.119.)

From living perception to abstract thought, *and from this to practice*—such is the dialectical path of the cognition of truth, of the cognition of objective reality. (LCW 38.171.)

Hence, in the building of socialism the development of society becomes a conscious process conducted by the masses of the people under the leadership of the proletariat and its party:

In the present epoch of the development of society, the responsibility of correctly knowing and changing the world has been placed by history upon the shoulders of the proletariat and its party. This process, the practice of changing the world, which is determined in accordance with scientific knowledge, has already reached a historic moment in the world and in China, a great moment unprecedented in human history, that is, the moment for completely banishing darkness from the world and for changing the world into a world of light such as never previously existed. The struggle of the proletariat and the revolutionary people to change the world comprises the fulfilment of the following tasks : to change the objective world and at the same time their own subjective world—to change their cognitive ability and change the relations between the subjective and the objective world. . . . And the objective world which is to be changed also includes all the opponents of change, who, in order to be changed, must go through a stage of compulsion before they can enter the stage of voluntary, conscious change. The epoch of world communism will be reached when all mankind voluntarily and consciously changes itself and the world. (MSW 1.308.)

Thus, the Party leadership and the rank-and-file, the Party and the proletariat, the proletariat and the rest of the people, the people and the reactionaries—these are four major contradictions underlying the movement of socialist society, each of them being included in the wider contradiction as its principal aspect. The first three are non-antagonistic by nature, though they may become antagonistic, if handled incorrectly; the fourth is antagonistic by nature, but, if handled correctly, will eventually become non-antagonistic; and then, when the transition to communism has been completed, all forms of state power, including democracy, dictatorship and the Party itself, will disappear :

When classes disappear, all instruments of class struggle—parties and the state machinery—will lose their function, cease to be necessary, therefore gradually wither away and end their historical mission; and human society will move to a higher stage . . .

Communists the world over are wiser than the bourgeoisie, they understand the laws governing the existence and development of things, they understand dialectics and they can see further. The bourgeoisie does not welcome this truth because it does not want to be overthrown. . . . But for the working class, the labouring people and the Communist Party the question is not one of being overthrown, but of working hard to create the conditions in which classes, state power and political parties will die out very naturally and mankind will enter the realm of Great Harmony. (MSW 4.411.)

CHAPTER VII

The First Socialist State

The history of all past society has consisted in the development of class antagonisms, antagonisms that assumed different forms at different epochs. But, whatsoever form they have taken, one fact is common to all past ages, namely, the exploitation of one part of society by the other.

—*Communist Manifesto*

1. *The Proletarian Revolution*

Summarising Lenin's analysis of the differences between the bourgeois and the proletarian revolution, Stalin wrote :

The distinction between the proletarian revolution and the bourgeois revolution may be reduced to five main points.

1. The bourgeois revolution usually begins when there exist more or less finished forms of the capitalist order, forms which have grown and ripened within the womb of feudal society prior to the open revolution; whereas the proletarian revolution begins when finished forms of the socialist order are either absent or almost completely absent.

2. The main task of the bourgeois revolution consists in seizing power and making it conform

to the already existing bourgeois economy, whereas the main task of the proletarian revolution consists in seizing power in order to build up a new socialist economy.

3. The bourgeois revolution is usually *consummated* with the seizure of power, whereas in the proletarian revolution the seizure of power is only the *beginning,* and power is used as a lever for transforming the old economy and organising the new one.

4. The bourgeois revolution limits itself to substituting one group of exploiters for another in the seat of power, and therefore it need not break up the old state machine; whereas the proletarian revolution removes all the exploiting groups from power and places in power the leader of all the toilers and exploited, the class of proletarians, in view of which it cannot abstain from breaking up the old state machine and replacing it with a new one.

5. The bourgeois revolution cannot rally the millions of the toiling and exploited masses for any length of time, for the very reason that they are toilers and exploited; whereas the proletarian revolution can and must join them, as toilers and exploited, in a durable alliance with the proletariat, if it wishes to carry out its main task of consolidating the power of the proletariat and building the new socialist economy. (SCW 8.22, cf. LCW 27.89.)

Thus, having overthrown the bourgeoisie, the proletariat is confronted with the task of constructing a new social order, which will differ not only from capitalism but from all previous forms of class society in that it brings exploitation to an end. It follows that the proletarian revolution involves more profound changes, and therefore greater difficulties, than any previous revolution.

Further, these difficulties, inherent in the nature of proletarian revolutions, were necessarily at their greatest in the October Revolution, because it was the first. After seizing power and defeating their enemies, internal and external, with a Red Army created in the thick of the fighting, the Russian workers and peasants turned to the task of building socialism with no experience to draw on, with no help from any friendly state, harassed by sabotage organised from abroad, and faced with the threat of renewed intervention.

The actual seizure of power had not been so difficult. This was due to the political situation created by the war. Internally, the backward economy of the Tsarist era had collapsed under the impact of military defeat. Externally, the imperialist powers, locked together as they were in mortal combat, were unable to intervene (LCW 27.92, SCW 6.162); and later, when they did intervene, they were hampered by the opposition of their own workers—revolutionary uprisings in Hungary and Germany, actions in support of the Bolsheviks in France and Britain (LCW 30.386, 33.145, SCW 6.391). Thanks to these political factors, the revolution survived. But then, as it passed from the struggle for power to socialist construction, the backwardness of Tsarism became a major obstacle :

> The more backward the country which, owing to the zigzags of history, has proved to be the one to start the socialist revolution, the more difficult it is for her to pass from the old capitalist relations to socialist relations. (LCW 27.89.)

In the West the reverse situation obtained. There, the socio-economic conditions of monopoly capitalism—large-scale production, universal literacy, and a high level of labour skill and trade-union organisation—were favourable to socialist construction; but, so long as the workers were held back by reformist illusions, the political conditions were lacking. Lenin pointed the contrast by comparing Russia with Germany :

Socialism is inconceivable without large-scale capitalist engineering based on the latest discoveries of modern science.... At the same time socialism is inconceivable unless the proletariat is the ruler of the state.... In 1918, Germany and Russia had become the most striking embodiment of the material realisation of the economic, productive and socio-economic conditions for socialism, on the one hand, and the political conditions, on the other. (LCW 32.334.)

Accordingly, Lenin argued that in the West the revolution would be slower in coming than it was in Russia but less difficult when it did come; and at the same time he warned the Bolsheviks not to be deceived by the ease with which they had won power, because their greatest difficulties lay ahead :

Anyone who has given careful thought to the economic requisites of the socialist revolution in Europe must be clear on the point that in Europe it will be immeasurably more difficult to start, whereas for us it was immeasurably easier to start; but it will be more difficult for us to continue the revolution than it will be over there. This objective situation has caused us to experience an extraordinarily sharp and difficult turn in history. (LCW 27.93.)

Looking at the Russian revolution as a whole, therefore, he concluded :

We began our revolution in unusually difficult conditions, such as no other workers' revolution in the world will ever have to face. (LCW 28.137.)

2. Socialist Construction

At the end of the civil war the economic life of the country was almost at a standstill, and the worker-peasant alliance was under a severe strain. The situation was only saved by Lenin's New Economic Policy, through which production was revived on the basis of private trade in small industry and agriculture. After this period of economic restoration the struggle for socialist construction began.

Industrialisation requires capital, and the only available source of capital was the labour of the proletariat and peasantry. Stalin said :

In the capitalist countries industrialisation was usually effected, in the main, by robbing other countries, by robbing colonies or defeated countries, or with the help of substantial and more or less enslaving loans from abroad.

You know that for hundreds of years Britain collected capital from all her colonies and from all parts of the world, and was able in this way to make additional investments in her industry. This incidentally explains why Britain became at one time the 'workshop of the world'.

You know also that Germany developed her industry with the help, among other things, of the 5,000 million francs which she levied as an indemnity on France after the Franco-Prussian war.

One respect in which our country differs from the capitalist countries is that we cannot and must not engage in colonial robbery, or in the plundering of other countries in general. That way, therefore, is closed to us.

Neither, however, does our country have, or want to have, enslaving loans from abroad. Consequently, that way too is closed to us.

What then remains? Only one thing, and that is to develop industry, to industrialise the country, with the help of *internal* accumulations. . . .

But what are the chief sources of these accumulations? As I have said, there are two such sources : first, the working class, which creates values and advances our industry; secondly, the peasantry.

The way matters stand with the peasantry in this respect is as follows. It not only pays the state the usual taxes, direct and indirect; it also *over-pays* in the relatively high prices for manufactured goods—that is in the first place—and it is more or less *under-paid* in the prices for agricultural produce—that is in the second place.

This is an additional tax levied on the peasantry for the sake of promoting industry, which caters for the whole country, the peasantry included. (SCW 11.165.)

In order to implement this policy it was necessary to maintain the dictatorship of the proletariat and the worker-peasant alliance, in which the masses of the peasantry joined with the proletariat in the struggle against the kulaks :

The alliance of the proletariat with the peasantry is an alliance of the working class with the labouring masses of the peasantry. Such an alliance cannot be effective without a struggle against capitalist elements in the peasantry, against the kulaks. Such an alliance cannot be a stable one unless the poor peasants are organised as the bulwark of the working class in the countryside. That is why the alliance between the workers and peasants under the present conditions of the dictatorship of the proletariat can be effected only in accordance with Lenin's well-known slogan : rely on the poor peasants, build a stable alliance with the middle peasants, and never cease fighting against the kulaks. For only by applying this slogan can the main mass of the peasantry be drawn into the channel of socialist construction. (SCW 11.101, cf. LCW 29.117.)

Under Stalin's leadership these tasks were accomplished. In a backward country, ruined by war and civil war, surrounded by enemies, a socialist state was created, the first in the world, with a modern industry, modern agriculture, and a modern army strong enough to withstand and destroy the armed might of fascist Germany, which had been built up by the imperialists for the express purpose of destroying socialism. For these reasons Stalin is assured of a place in history by the side of Lenin.

3. 'Left' and Right Deviations

Besides the difficulties inherent in the objective situation, there were others arising from the lack of unity in the subjective forces of the revolution. For many years the leadership was openly divided. The Leninists, led by Lenin and later by Stalin, were opposed by several groups, led by Trotsky, Bukharin and others, who were often divided among themselves but at one in their opposition to Lenin and Stalin. Two main lines of opposition emerged, one led by Trotsky, who maintained that, unless there was a revolution in the West, the Soviet republic was bound to collapse, and the other by Bukharin, who maintained that the kulaks should not be coerced but allowed to 'grow peacefully into socialism'. These two lines exemplify the 'Left' and Right forms of opportunism, which have been discussed in Chapter I.

In 1905, when Lenin formulated his theory of 'uninterrupted revolution', Trotsky put forward in opposition to it his own theory of 'permanent revolution', borrowing the name from Marx. According to this theory, the proletariat, having overthrown the Tsar, will find itself in conflict with the masses of the peasantry and will be unable to maintain itself in power without state support from the proletariat of the West, that is, without a proletarian revolution in the West. In keeping with this theory, Trotsky refused to conclude the peace negotiations at Brest-Litovsk, on the ground that to make peace with the German imperialists would be to betray the coming revolution in Germany. This was described by Lenin as a 'strange and monstrous' decision (LCW 27.68); and, if he had not succeeded in reversing it, the Soviet republic would undoubtedly have collapsed.

Of course, Lenin recognised that the revolution in Russia might fail; but he maintained that, even if it did fail, it would still mark an advance in the world revolution, and that it was only through a series of such attempts, none of them completely successful, that the ultimate victory of world socialism would be secured:

We are not in a position to call forth at will a socialist revolution in the West, which is the only absolute guarantee against restoration in Russia. But a relative and conditional 'guarantee', that is, one that would raise the greatest possible *obstacles* to restoration, lies in carrying out the revolution in Russia in the most far-reaching, consistent and determined manner possible. The more far-reaching the revolution is, the more difficult it will be to restore the old order and the more gains will remain even if restoration does take place. (LCW 13.327.)

It would be a fatal mistake to declare that, since there is a discrepancy between our economic 'forces' and our political strength, it 'follows' that we should not have seized power. Such an argument can be advanced only by a 'man in a muffler', who forgets that there will always be such a 'discrepancy', that it always exists in the development of nature and society alike, and that only by a series of attempts—each of which, taken by itself, will be one-sided and suffer from certain inconsistencies—will complete socialism be created by the revolutionary co-operation of the proletarians of *all* countries. (LCW 32.339.)

It will be seen that, apart from the name, Trotsky's theory of 'permanent revolution' has nothing in common with Marx's theory except the idea of 'simultaneity', which proved in the event to be mistaken. Trotsky failed to distinguish the two stages of the revolution and denied a revolutionary role to the peasantry. This was the Menshevik position. Like the Mensheviks, he failed to see that the differentiation of the peasantry after 1905 was making them more, not less, revolutionary; for the peasant masses were being drawn closer to the urban proletariat, and at the same time the struggle against Tsarism, which involved the entire peasantry, was becoming more acute :

This task is being wrongly tackled in *Nashe Slovo* by Trotsky, who is repeating his 'original' 1905 theory and refuses to give some thought to the reason why, in the course of ten years, life has been by-passing this splendid theory of his.

From the Bolsheviks Trotsky's original theory has borrowed their call for a decisive proletarian revolutionary struggle, while from the Mensheviks it has borrowed 'repudiation' of the role of the peasantry. . . .

A whole decade—the great decade of 1905-15—has shown the existence of two, and only two, class lines in the Russian revolution. The differentiation of the peasantry has enhanced the class struggle within them; it has aroused many hitherto politically dormant elements. It has drawn the rural proletariat closer to the urban proletariat. . . . However, the antagonism between the peasantry, on the one hand, and the Markovs, Romanovs and Khvostovs, on the other, has become stronger and more acute. This is such an obvious truth that not even the thousands of phrases in the scores of Trotsky's Paris articles will 'refute' it. Trotsky is in fact helping the liberal-labour politicians in Russia, who by 'repudiation' of the role of the peasantry understand a *refusal* to rouse the peasants for the revolution. (LCW 21.419-20.)

Lenin's opinion of Trotsky's theoretical and political line may be seen in the following comments :

Trotsky distorts Bolshevism, because he has never been able to form any definite views on the role of the proletariat in the Russian bourgeois revolution. (LCW 16.380.)

And that fact proves we were right in calling Trotsky a representative of the 'worst remnants of factionalism'. . . .

Under cover of 'non-factionalism' Trotsky is championing the interests of a group abroad which particularly lacks definite principles and has no basis in the working-class movement in Russia.

All that glitters is not gold. There is much glitter and sound in Trotsky's phrases, but they are meaningless. (LCW 20.332.)

Trotsky has never yet held a firm opinion on any

important question of Marxism. He always contrives to worm his way into the cracks of any difference of opinion, and desert one side for the other. (LCW 20.447.)

In a letter dated February 19, 1917, he wrote :

Trotsky arrived, and this scoundrel at once ganged up with the *right* wing of *Novy Mir* against the Left Zimmerwaldists ! ! That's it ! ! That's Trotsky for you ! ! always true to himself—twists, swindles, poses as a left, *helps* the right, so long as he can . . . (LCW 35.288, cf. 285.)

At the end of 1920 Trotsky produced a pamphlet in which he attacked the Party line on developing trade union democracy. Lenin criticised it as follows :

My principal material is Comrade Trotsky's pamphlet, *The Role and Tasks of the Trade Unions.* When I compare it with the theses he submitted to the Central Committee, and go over it very carefully, I am amazed at the number of theoretical mistakes and glaring blunders it contains. . . .

He has, I am quite sure, made a number of mistakes bearing on the very essence of the dictatorship of the proletariat. (LCW 32.19-22, cf. 36.595.)

In 1930, fighting for the Leninist line against both 'Left' and Right deviations, Stalin made the following analysis of Trotskyism :

What is the essence of Trotskyism?

The essence of Trotskyism is, first of all, denial of the possibility of completely building socialism in the U.S.S.R. by the efforts of the working class and peasantry of our country. What does this mean? It means that, if a victorious world revolution does not come to our aid in the near future, we shall have to surrender to the bourgeoisie and clear the way for a bourgeois-democratic republic. Consequently, we have here the bourgeois denial of the possibility of completely building socialism in our country, disguised by 'revolutionary' phrases about the victory of the world revolution. . . .

The essence of Trotskyism is, secondly, denial of the possibility of drawing the main mass of the peasantry into the work of socialist construction in the countryside. What does this mean? It means that the working class is incapable of leading the peasantry in the work of transferring the individual peasant farms to collectivist lines, that, if the victory of the world revolution does not come to the aid of the working class in the near future, the peasantry will restore the old bourgeois order. . . .

The essence of Trotskyism is, lastly, denial of the necessity for iron discipline in the Party, recognition of freedom for factional groupings in the Party, recognition of the need to form a Trotskyist party. According to Trotskyism, the C.P.S.U.(B.) must not be a single, united militant party, but a collection of groups and factions, each with its own centre, its own discipline, its own press, and so forth. What does this mean? It means proclaiming freedom for political factions in the Party. It means that freedom for political groupings in the Party must be followed by freedom for political parties in the country, that is, bourgeois democracy. . . .

Capitulation in practice as the *content*, 'Left' phrases and revolutionary adventurist postures as the *form*, disguising and advertising the defeatist *content*—such is the essence of Trotskyism.

This duality of Trotskyism reflects the duality in the position of the urban petty bourgeoisie, which is being ruined, cannot tolerate the 'regime' of the dictatorship of the proletariat and is striving either to jump into socialism 'at one go' in order to avoid being ruined (hence *adventurism* and *hysterics* in policy), or, if this is impossible, to make every conceivable concession to capitalism (hence *capitulation* in policy). (SCW 12.364.)

At the same congress Stalin analysed the Right deviation, led by Bukharin, Rykov and Tomsky:

It cannot be said that the Right deviators do not admit the possibility of completely building socialism in the U.S.S.R. No, they do admit it, and that distinguishes them from the Trotskyists. But the misfortune of the Right deviators is that, while formally admitting that it is possible to build socialism in one country, they refuse to recognise the ways and means of struggle without which it is impossible to build socialism.... They think that socialism can be built on the quiet, automatically, without class struggle, without an offensive against the capitalist elements. They think that the capitalist elements will either die out imperceptibly or else grow into socialism. Since, however, such miracles do not happen in history, it follows that the Right deviators are in fact slipping into the viewpoint of denying the possibility of completely building socialism in our country.

Nor can it be said that the Right deviators deny that it is possible to draw the main mass of the peasantry into the work of building socialism in the countryside. No, they admit that it is possible, and that distinguishes them from the Trotskyists. But, while admitting it formally, they will not accept the ways and means without which it is impossible to draw the peasantry into the work of building socialism.... They think that the chief thing now is not a high rate of industrial development, and not collective farms and state farms, but to 'release' the elemental forces of the market, to 'emancipate' the market and to 'remove the shackles' from the individual farms, up to and including those of the capitalist elements in the countryside. Since, however, the kulaks cannot grow into socialism, and 'emancipating' the market means arming the kulaks and disarming the working class, it follows that the Right deviators are in fact slipping into the viewpoint of denying that it is possible to draw the main mass of the peasantry into the work of building socialism. . . .

The Right deviators do not take the stand of forming another party, and that is another thing that distinguishes them from the Trotskyists. The leaders of the Right deviators have openly admitted their mistakes and have surrendered to the Party. But it would be foolish to think on these grounds that the Right deviation is already buried. The strength of Right opportunism is not measured by this circumstance. The strength of Right opportunism lies in the strength of the petty-bourgeois elemental forces, in the strength of the pressure on the Party exercised by the capitalist elements in general and by the kulaks in particular. . . .

That is how matters stand as regards the 'Left' and Right deviations in the Party.

The task is to continue the uncompromising struggle *on two fronts,* against the 'Lefts', who represent *petty-bourgeois radicalism*, and against the Rights, who represent *petty-bourgeois liberalism*. (SCW 12.364-72.)

It only remains to add that in professing to admit their mistakes the Rightists were guilty of deception. It was subsequently shown at the Moscow trials that both groups were working for the counter-revolution.

4. The New Bourgeoisie

The proletarian revolution puts an end to exploitation, but not to class struggle. Even after the collectivisation of agriculture, there remains a contradiction in the economic base between the collective farms, which are owned by the collective, and the state farms, which are state-owned. Within the collective, each family has its own holding, with the right to sell its produce on the open market. Thus, the peasantry is still tied to small commodity production. So, too, are the handicraft-workers. The proletariat enjoys a higher standard of living than the peasantry, corresponding to the division between town and country, which has been inherited from capitalist society. In industry itself there is a contradiction between the collective character of labour and the individual character of wages. The capitalists, landowners and kulaks have been expropriated, but they are still active, many of them being employed in the government and public services.

Lenin warned repeatedly that, apart from the danger of foreign intervention, there still existed within the Soviet system conditions giving rise to the possibility of a capitalist restoration :

> The transition from capitalism to communism takes an entire historical epoch. Until this epoch is over, the exploiters inevitably cherish the hope of restoration, and this *hope* turns into *attempts* at restoration. (LCW 28.254.)

> The bourgeoisie are emerging, not only from among our Soviet government employees—only a very few can emerge from their ranks—but from the ranks of the peasants and handicraftsmen. . . . It shows that even in Russia capitalist commodity production is alive, operating, developing and giving

rise to a bourgeoisie, just as it does in every capitalist society. (LCW 29.189)

As long as we live in a small-peasant country, there is a surer economic basis for capitalism in Russia than for communism. This must be borne in mind. Anyone who has carefully observed life in the countryside, as compared with life in the towns, knows that we have not torn out the roots of capitalism and have not undermined the foundation, the basis, of the internal enemy. The latter depends on small-scale production, and there is only one way of undermining it, namely, to place the economy of the country, including agriculture, on a new technical basis, the technical basis of modern large-scale production. (LCW 31.516.)

Lenin's warning was repeated by Stalin :

Have we in our Soviet country any of the conditions that would make the restoration of capitalism *possible*? Yes, we have. That, comrades, may appear strange, but it is a fact. We have overthrown capitalism, we have established the dictatorship of the proletariat, we are developing our socialist industry at a rapid pace and are linking peasant economy with it. But we have not yet torn out the roots of capitalism. Where are these roots imbedded? They are imbedded in commodity production, in small production in the towns and especially the countryside. (SCW 11.235.)

This new bourgeoisie could not work openly—except abroad, where the émigrés were very active and well-organised—but it had its own ideology, known as Smena-Vekhism, which Stalin described as follows :

Smena-Vekhism is the ideology of the new bourgeoisie, which is growing and little by little linking up with the kulaks and the intelligentsia in the government service. The new bourgeoisie has put forward its own ideology, the Smena-Vekh ideology, which consists in the view that the Communist Party is bound to degenerate and the new bourgeoisie to consolidate itself, while it appears that, without ourselves noticing it, we Bolsheviks are bound to reach the threshold of the democratic republic, then to cross that threshold, and, with the assistance of some 'Caesar', who will come forward, perhaps from the ranks of the military or perhaps from the government service officials, to find ourselves in the position of an ordinary bourgeois republic. (SCW 7.350.)

The progress of our industry, the progress of our trading and co-operative bodies, the improvement of our state apparatus, is progress and improvement of benefit to the working class, of benefit to the main mass of the peasantry, but of disadvantage to the new bourgeoisie, of disadvantage to the middle strata generally and to the urban middle strata in particular. Is it to be wondered at that discontent with the Soviet regime is growing among these strata? Hence the counter-revolutionary moods in these circles. Hence the Smena-Vekhist ideology as a fashionable commodity on the political market of the new bourgeoisie. (SCW 10.325.)

One of the most effective weapons in the hands of the new bourgeoisie was bureaucracy. This was one of the evils inherited from the old regime :

Under capitalism, democracy is restricted, cramped, curtailed, mutilated by all the conditions of wage-slavery and the poverty and misery of the people. This, and this alone, is the reason why the functionaries of our political organisations and trade unions are corrupted—or rather tend to be corrupted—by the conditions of capitalism and betray a tendency to become bureaucrats, that is, privileged persons divorced from the people and standing *above* the people. That is the *essence* of bureaucracy, and until the capitalists have been expropriated and the bourgeoisie overthrown, even proletarian functionaries will inevitably be 'bureaucratised' to a certain extent. (LCW 25.486.)

The training of new proletarian administrators was necessarily a slow process, and meanwhile many of the old officials had to be retained. Many of these were secretly hostile to the new regime, and all of them clung to the old methods and values :

We now have a vast army of government employees, but lack sufficiently educated forces to exercise real control over them. In practice it often happens that here at the top, where we exercise political power, the machine functions somehow.... Down below, however, there are hundreds of thousands of old officials, whom we took over from the Tsar and from bourgeois society, and who, in part deliberately and in part unwittingly, work against us. (LCW 33.428, cf. 29.32.)

When we are told ... that the state farms everywhere are hiding-places for old landowners slightly disguised or not disguised at all, and that similar things are often to be observed in chief administration and central boards, I never doubt that it is true. (LCW 30.245.)

Stalin drew attention to the same evil in even sharper terms :

I am referring to the bureaucratic elements to be found in our party, government, trade-union, co-operative and all other organisations. I am referring to the bureaucratic elements who batten on our weaknesses and errors, who fear like the plague all criticism by the masses, all control by the masses, and hinder us in developing self-criticism and ridding ourselves of our weaknesses and errors. Bureaucracy in our organisations must not be regarded merely as routine and red tape. Bureaucracy is a manifestation of bourgeois influence on our organisations. (SCW 11.137, cf. LCW 32.191.)

The danger was all the greater because, owing to the shortage of cadres, bureaucratic practices were penetrating into the Party itself :

It was only to be expected that red tape in the Soviet apparatus would penetrate into the Party apparatus, because the two are intimately interwoven. (LCW 31.435, cf. 421, SCW 6.10.)

The key feature is that we have not got the right men in the right places; that responsible Communists, who acquitted themselves magnificently during the revolution, have been given commercial and industrial functions about which they know nothing; and they prevent us from seeing the truth, for rogues and rascals hide themselves magnificently behind their backs. (LCW 33.304.)

All shrewd whiteguards are definitely banking on the fact that the alleged proletarian character of our Party does not in the least safeguard it against the small-proprietor elements gaining predominance in it, and very rapidly too. (LCW 33.254, cf. 187, 31.115.)

All the work of all our economic bodies suffers most of all from bureaucracy. Communists have become bureaucrats. If anything will destroy us, it is this. (LCW 35.549, cf. 32.24, 56.)

Even when it did not serve as a screen for counter-revolutionaries, bureaucracy was dangerous, because, by placing administration above politics, it alienated the masses from the Party, and so undermined the basis of the dictatorship of the proletariat :

The task is to learn to organise the work properly, not to lag behind, to remove friction in time, not to separate administration from politics; for our administration and our politics rest on the ability of the entire vanguard to maintain contact with the entire mass of the proletariat and the entire mass of the peasantry. If anyone forgets these cogs and becomes wholly absorbed in administration, the result will be disastrous. (LCW 33.299.)

In the sea of the people we are after all but a drop in the ocean, and we can administer only when we express correctly what the people are conscious of. Unless we can do this, the Communist Party will not lead the proletariat, the proletariat will not lead the masses, and the whole machine will collapse. (LCW 33.304.)

In considering the problem of bureaucracy, Lenin had little patience with those who, like Trotsky, treated it as though it could be solved by speech-making :

It will take decades to overcome the evils of bureaucracy. It is a very difficult struggle, and anyone who says we can rid ourselves of bureaucratic practices overnight by adopting anti-bureaucratic platforms is nothing but a quack with a bent for fine words. (LCW 32.56, cf. 68, 89, 33.428, 481.)

5. The Need for a Cultural Revolution

What made the struggle against bureaucracy so difficult was that it had to be conducted simultaneously in the economic basis and in the ideological superstructure. On the one hand, being rooted in small commodity production, it could not be completely eradicated until the whole economy had been reconstructed on the basis of large-scale socialist production; on the other, it was itself one of the main obstacles to economic reconstruction—an obstacle which, if not removed, might reverse the whole process.

Lenin understood that the key to the problem lay with the masses. If the masses could be aroused to take the initiative in developing production, working not for private gain but for the common good, they would both overcome in themselves the ideological obstacles inherited from the old society and recognise the need to take the work of administration into their own hands.

In regard to production, the masses had already demonstrated their initiative in the subbotniks. During the civil war, when Kolchak's armies were threatening to overwhelm the young Soviet republic, the railway workers of Moscow organised teams for voluntary overtime labour in the railway yards; and within a few weeks the movement spread like wildfire to all the principal railway centres and to other industries. Greeting these workers, Lenin said :

Evidently this is only a beginning, but it is a beginning of exceptionally great importance. It is the beginning of a revolution which is more difficult, more tangible, more radical, more decisive than the overthrow of the bourgeoisie; for it is a victory over our own conservatism, indiscipline, petty-bourgeois egoism, a victory over habits left as a heritage to the workers and peasants by accursed capitalism. Only when *this* victory has been consolidated will the new social discipline, socialist discipline, be created; then, and only then, will a reversion to capitalism become impossible and communism become really invincible. (LCW 29.411.)

In regard to administration, it was of course necessary for the workers to raise their educational and cultural level, but that in itself was not enough. If they were to put an end to bureaucracy, it was necessary that they should themselves participate in the work of government. Only then would the Soviet system become government *by,* and not merely *for,* the people. Speaking at the Eighth Party Congress (1919), Lenin said:

We can fight bureaucracy to the bitter end, to complete victory, only when the whole population participates in the work of government. In the bourgeois republics not only is this impossible, but *the law itself prevents it.* The best of the bourgeois republics, no matter how democratic they may be, have thousands of legal hindrances which prevent people from participating in the work of government. What we have done is to remove these hindrances, but so far we have not reached the stage at which the working people could participate in government. Apart from the law, there is still the level of culture, which you cannot subject to any law. The result of this low cultural level is that the Soviets, which in virtue of their programme are organs of government *by* the working people, are in fact organs of government *for* the working people by the advanced section of the proletariat, not by the working people as a whole. . . .

Bureaucracy has been defeated. The exploiters have been eliminated. But the cultural level has not been raised, and therefore the bureaucrats are still occupying their old positions. They can be forced to retreat only if the proletariat and peasantry are organised far more extensively than they have been hitherto, and only if real measures are taken to enlist the workers in government. (LCW 29.183.)

Lenin returned to this theme at the Eleventh Congress (1922)—the last that he attended; and early in 1923, in one of his last articles, he issued a call for a 'cultural revolution':

> Our opponents have told us repeatedly that we were rash in undertaking to implant socialism in an insufficiently cultured country. They were misled by the fact of our having started from the opposite end to the one prescribed by theory—the theory of pedants of all kinds. In our country the political and social revolution preceded the cultural revolution, that same cultural revolution which nevertheless confronts us now. (LCW 33.474.)

Lenin's call was repeated by Stalin:

> The surest remedy for bureaucracy is raising the cultural level of the workers and peasants. One can curse and denounce bureaucracy in the state apparatus, one can stigmatise and pillory bureaucracy in our practical work; but, unless the masses of the workers reach a certain level of culture, which will create the possibility, the desire, the ability, to control the state apparatus, bureaucracy will continue to exist in spite of everything. Therefore, the cultural development of the working class and of the masses of the working peasantry, not only the development of literacy—although literacy is the basis of all culture—but primarily the cultivation of the ability to take part in the administration of the country, is the chief lever for improving the state and every other apparatus. This is the sense and significance of Lenin's slogan about the cultural revolution. (SCW 10.330, cf. 11.40.)

Lastly, our economic organisations. . . . How are we to put an end to bureaucracy in all these organisations? There is only one sole way of doing this, and that is to organise control from below, to organise criticism of the bureaucracy in our institutions, of their shortcomings and mistakes, by the vast masses of the working class. (SCW 11.77.)

Granted the need for a cultural revolution, . what form was it to take? This problem was not solved. The Soviet workers and peasants had succeeded, in the face of almost insuperable difficulties, in building their own state; but, for the reasons given, they did not succeed in bringing it completely under their control.

6. *The Class Struggle in Socialist Society*

In February 1931 Stalin uttered this prophetic warning:

We are fifty or a hundred years behind the advanced countries. We must make good this distance in ten years. Either we do it, or we go under. (SCW 13.41.)

Two years later the Nazis seized power in Germany. Rather than face the possibility of a Communist majority in parliament, the German monopoly capitalists, supported by other monopoly capitalists of the West, discarded the bourgeois parliamentary system, which had served them hitherto as a screen, and installed an open dictatorship in preparation for what was to be the final confrontation with the Soviet Union. It is against this background of intensive war preparations that Stalin's handling of internal class contradictions must be judged.

In 1933 the first five-year plan was completed; in

1937 the second five-year plan was completed. The difficulties were immense—inexperience, incompetence, and above all sabotage; yet they were all overcome, thanks to what Lenin had called 'mass heroism in plain, everyday work' (LCW 29.423).

In January 1933, reviewing the results of the first five-year plan, Stalin said :

> We must bear in mind that the growth of the power of the Soviet state will intensify the resistance of the last remnants of the dying classes. It is precisely because they are dying and their days are numbered that they will go on from one form of attack to another, sharper form, appealing to the backward sections of the population and mobilising them against the Soviet regime. (SCW 13.216.)

A year later, reviewing the progress of the second five-year plan, he said :

> But can we say that we have already overcome all the survivals of capitalism in economic life? No, we cannot say that. Still less can we say that we have overcome the survivals of capitalism in people's minds. We cannot say that, not only because the development of people's minds trails behind their economic position, but because we are still surrounded by capitalist countries, which are trying to revive and sustain the survivals of capitalism in economic life and in the minds of the people of the U.S.S.R., and against which we Bolsheviks must always keep our powder dry.
>
> It stands to reason that these survivals cannot but create a favourable soil for the revival of the ideology of the defeated anti-Leninist groups in the minds of individual members of our Party. . . .
>
> That is why we cannot say that the fight is ended

and that there is no longer any need for the policy of the socialist offensive. (SCW 13.356.)

Thus, according to these two statements, the remnants of the exploiting classes, supported by the capitalist powers, were still endeavouring to mobilise backward sections of the Soviet people against the regime. The class struggle was not only continuing but growing sharper.

In 1936 a new constitution was adopted, which guaranteed equal rights for all, 'irrespective of race, nationality, religion, standard of education, domicile, social origin, property status, or past activities'. It was, as Stalin claimed, the most democratic constitution in the world. Introducing it in November of that year, he said:

> The landlord class, as you know, had already been eliminated as a result of the victorious conclusion of the civil war. As for the other exploiting classes, they have shared the fate of the landlord class. The capitalist class in the sphere of industry has ceased to exist. The kulak class in the sphere of agriculture has ceased to exist. And the merchants and profiteers in the sphere of trade have ceased to exist. Thus, all the exploiting classes have now been eliminated. (SL 565.)

> The draft of the new Constitution of the U.S.S.R. proceeds from the fact that there are no longer any antagonistic classes in society. . . . (SL 571.)

Here the exploiting classes have been eliminated; the class struggle, it would seem, is at an end.

In March 1937, calling for greater vigilance within the Party in defending it from infiltration by counter-revolutionary agents, Stalin said:

> It is necessary to shatter and discard the rotten theory to the effect that with every step of progress

that we make the class struggle here is bound to die more and more, that in proportion to the growth of our successes the class enemy becomes more and more tamed. . . .

On the contrary, the greater our progress, the greater our successes, the more embittered the remnants of the smashed exploiting classes will become, the more quickly they will resort to sharper forms of struggle, the more they will do damage to the Soviet state, the more they will clutch at the most desperate means of struggle as the last resort of the doomed.

We must bear in mind that the remnants of the routed classes in the U.S.S.R. are not alone. They have direct support from our enemies beyond the borders of the U.S.S.R. It would be a mistake to suppose that the sphere of the class struggle is bounded by the frontiers of the U.S.S.R. While one end of the class struggle operates within the U.S.S.R., its other end extends into the bourgeois states around us. (SMT 262.)

Here the class struggle is again envisaged as continuing and growing more acute.

Finally, in his report to the Eighteenth Party Congress in March 1939, Stalin said :

While capitalist society is torn by irreconcilable contradictions between workers and capitalists and between peasants and landlords—resulting in its internal instability—Soviet society, liberated from the yoke of exploitation, knows no such contradictions, is free of class conflicts, and presents a picture of friendly collaboration between workers, peasants and intellectuals. (SL 645.)

Here Soviet society is again presented as being free of class antagonisms.

How are these discrepancies to be explained? Before

attempting to answer this question, we must consider the measures taken during these years to defeat the counter-revolutionary forces.

On the one hand, a number of political leaders, including Bukharin, Rykov and Zinoviev, also several army generals and a chief of police, were tried and convicted of treason and executed. Common to all these was the conviction that in the coming war a German victory was inevitable. In addition, a large number of spies and other enemy agents were eliminated. There can be little doubt that, if these measures had not been taken, the Soviet Union would have been destroyed. On the other hand, in the course of their counter-espionage activities, the security police, who were subject to no effective control, arrested on false charges many tens of thousands of innocent persons, and large numbers of these were executed without trial. These repressive measures were directed not so much against the workers and peasants, who were relatively unaffected, as against the intelligentsia and above all the Party itself. Not only did a large proportion of the victims consist of Party members, but many of these were among Stalin's most loyal supporters. The only intelligible explanation of these events is the one that was current at the time and subsequently endorsed at the Twentieth Party Congress (1956). Enemy agents had penetrated into the higher ranks of the security police. Stalin accepted responsibility for the purges, and admitted that they had been accompanied by 'grave mistakes' (SL 649). They show how narrow was the margin by which the counter-revolution failed.

These criminal violations of civic rights stand in flagrant contradiction to the new constitution, in which those rights were guaranteed; and this contradiction is clearly related to the contradiction already noted in Stalin's analysis of the state of classes in

Soviet society. Returning to his analysis, we ask, what was the actual situation? Was the class struggle growing more acute, or was it dying away?

During these years a new socialist economy had been constructed. Capitalist ownership had been replaced by socialist ownership, small-scale production by large-scale production. But the socialist transformation of the political and ideological superstructure still remained to be carried through. A new state apparatus had been created, controlled through the Party by the proletariat, but the masses were not yet fully involved in it. On the contrary, it had become to some extent alienated from the masses through the bureaucratic practices of bourgeois officials who occupied privileged positions in it. Bureaucratic tendencies were also growing in the Party itself. The old exploiting classes had been expropriated, but by no means eliminated. Many former landowners and capitalists had found employment in the public services, and former kulaks had joined the collective farms. These people had lost their property, but not their traditions and habits and outlook on life. The masses of the peasants in the collective farms still retained the mentality of the small proprietor. The proletariat itself had met the needs of industrial development by recruiting large numbers from the peasantry, and these too brought with them their petty-bourgeois prejudices. Thanks to the rapid expansion of the educational system, the masses had raised their cultural level, and illiteracy had been almost entirely abolished, but this still fell short of the cultural revolution which Lenin had regarded as necessary in order to involve the masses in the work of government. For these reasons, the final issue of the class struggle had still to be fought out, and, if the proletariat should relax its leadership, the expropriated classes would redouble their efforts to recover what they had lost.

A study of Stalin's speeches to Party cadres during this period shows that he was keenly aware of the danger that the Party might allow its ties with the masses to be corroded by 'bureaucratic rust' (SMT 278). He saw the danger and warned them repeatedly against it, but, perhaps because he was himself inclined to rely too much on 'pure administration' (LCW 36.606), he was unable to prevent it; and it was through this weakness in the socialist defences that the enemy found his way in. If the masses had been roused to take the class struggle into their own hands and carry it through to the end, taking care to distinguish between friends and enemies, they would have been able to isolate the counter-revolutionaries in their midst and at the same time to provide a check on the activities of the security police.

The answer to our question, therefore, is that, far from dying away, the resistance of the expropriated classes was continuing and assuming new forms, which were more insidious than the old and therefore even more dangerous. In these circumstances, it was vitally necessary to maintain and strengthen the dictatorship of the proletariat, as Lenin had foreseen.

From all this it may be concluded that Stalin followed the Leninist line down to 1935, but that subsequently, as the pressure of capitalist encirclement increased, he departed from it in two ways. On the one hand, the new constitution rested on the assumption that, so far as internal relations were concerned, the dictatorship of the proletariat could be relaxed; and for this reason it was welcomed by the new bourgeoisie, who accepted it as a confirmation of their privileges. This was a Right deviation. On the other hand, since the dictatorship of the proletariat could not in fact be relaxed, it was maintained by administrative methods as a function of the security police (SCW 13.160). This was a 'Left' deviation—the error of what Lenin had called 'over-administration'—which had already manifested itself in the leftist excesses that had marred the struggle against the kulaks (SCW 12.368). The two deviations complemented and supported one another. Enemies were treated as friends and friends as enemies.

In this connection, it is noteworthy that in his *Dialectical and Historical Materialism* (1938), Stalin did not distinguish between antagonistic and non-antagonistic contradictions, nor did he point out that, according as they are handled, antagonistic contradictions may become non-antagonistic and non-antagonistic contradictions may become antagonistic. This is one of the points at which Mao Tse-tung's treatment of dialectics marks an important advance.

7. *The New Revisionism*

As the Soviet Union grew stronger, the contradictions among the imperialist powers became more acute. They were united in their hostility to the first socialist state, divided in the face of its increasing might. This division was reflected in each country within the ruling class. In Britain, the section represented by Chamberlain, then in the majority, was encouraging Hitler to attack the Soviet Union in the hope that he would both destroy socialism and weaken himself in the process, so that Britain would emerge as the strongest power in Europe. Stalin offered Britain and France a mutual security pact, which, had it been accepted, would have prevented the war. When it became clear that it was not going to be accepted, he signed a non-aggression pact with Hitler, who then attacked in the West, and later overran the Balkans, thus threatening British interests in the Middle East. Meanwhile Chamberlain had been replaced by Churchill, who represented that section of the ruling class which regarded Hitler as the more immediate enemy. Having strengthened his position in the West, Hitler was now ready to attack in the East, and made a bid for British support; but Churchill replied by ranging Britain, with the support of the British people, on the side of the Soviet Union. This did not mean that the British ruling class had abandoned its objective. Only its tactics had changed. Churchill's aim was to give the Soviet Union such support as would enable her to defeat Germany, thereby exhausting herself and leaving Britain as the real victor. Once more they miscalculated. The Soviet people suffered incalculable losses—fifteen million dead, twenty-five million homeless, material damage exceeding the output of two five-year plans; but they won. The first socialist state had saved the world from fascism and opened the way for the last stage of imperialism—the stage of its final collapse.

Meanwhile, however, the internal contradictions remained. They might have been resolved, if there had been a call to the masses to complete the victory over the external enemy by defending the dictatorship of the proletariat against those who were undermining it from within; but that call was not given. Faced with a renewal of imperialist pressure, bringing the threat of a new war, Stalin resorted to the same measures as before—further concessions to the new bourgeoisie combined with further repression. It may be that, after twenty-five years, his powers of leadership were failing. No other statesman in history had carried so heavy a burden for so long.

The bureaucracy was now entrenching itself as a privileged class, cut off from the workers and peasants by a large and growing income gap. Some flagrant cases of bourgeois corruption were exposed at the Nineteenth Party Congress (1952). After Stalin's death in 1953 there was a struggle for power, resulting in the arrest and execution of Beria, who had been in charge of the security police since 1938; and the leadership then passed into the hands of the new bourgeoisie, represented by Khrushchev.

Khrushchev's aim was to establish the new bourgeoisie as the ruling class in a system of bureaucratic state capitalism. He did not, of course, formulate his policy in these terms but, following the example of Bernstein and Kautsky, presented it in the form of a series of 'amendments' to Marxism.

According to Marxism-Leninism, the form of state which must necessarily prevail during the transition from capitalism to communism—that is, throughout the period of socialism—is the dictatorship of the proletariat. According to Khrushchev and the new revisionists, the dictatorship of the proletariat had ceased to exist in the Soviet Union and had been replaced by a 'state of the whole people'. This concept is alien to Marxism. According to Marxism, the only alternative to the dictatorship of the proletariat in modern society is the dictatorship of the bourgeoisie, and that is what Khrushchev's 'state of the whole people' really is.

According to Marxism-Leninism, the dictatorship of the proletariat is the highest form of democracy, since it is a dictatorship of the majority over the minority. According to Khrushchev and the new revisionists, the 'state of the whole people' is more democratic than the dictatorship of the proletariat, because it extends democracy to the whole people. This concept of, a classless democracy has no place in Marxism. It is a bourgeois concept, which Khrushchev adopted in order to conceal the fact that his 'state of the whole people' was really a dictatorship of the bourgeoisie.

According to Marxism-Leninism, the dictatorship of the proletariat is established and maintained under the leadership of the Communist Party, which, equipped with the revolutionary theory of Marxism-Leninism, acts as a vanguard of the working class. Under the leadership of Khrushchev and the new revisionists, the Communist Party of the Soviet Union has ceased to be a vanguard party of the working class, leading the struggle to consolidate the dictatorship of the proletariat, and become a 'party of the whole people', that is, a party whose function is to maintain the dictatorship of the bourgeoisie.

According to Marxism-Leninism, the dictatorship of the proletariat must be maintained and consolidated, not only to complete the work of socialist construction, but to re-educate the workers in a spirit of socialist discipline, eliminating all forms of bourgeois individualism in preparation for the transition to communism. This was the spirit of the subbotnik movement and of socialist emulation, in which, under the leadership of Lenin and Stalin, the workers had performed miracles of collective labour. Under the leadership of Khrushchev and the new revisionists, this spirit has been abandoned in favour of 'material incentives'; and at the same time it is claimed that Soviet society is advancing to communism. According to Marxism, the advance from socialism to communism requires that each worker's share of the social product should be proportionate, not to his work, but to his needs (LCW 25.472), in accordance with the principle 'all for each and each for all' (LCW 31.124). The advance cannot be made on the basis of material incentives, which represent the competitive element in wage-labour derived from bourgeois society (ME 2.23).

According to Marxism-Leninism, the ruling class rules by force, and therefore cannot be overthrown except by force. In the colonies the imperialists have always ruled by open force; in the metropolitan countries they have usually concealed the use of force beneath parliamentary forms; but, faced with a real threat to their privileges, they have always been ready to declare a 'state of emergency' and resort to open force. This is what every ruling class has always done :

> Major questions in the life of nations are settled only by force. The reactionary classes themselves are usually the first to resort to violence, to civil war; they are the first to 'place the bayonet on the agenda' ... (LCW 9.132.)

According to Khrushchev and the new revisionists, the possibilities are growing of the transition from capitalism to socialism being effected peacefully by parliamentary means. There is not a single socialist country in which the transition has been effected in this way; but there are several capitalist countries in which, disarmed by the illusion of 'peaceful transition', the workers' movement has been crushed.

At all these points Khrushchev and the new revisionists have abandoned the Marxist-Leninist theory of the dictatorship of the proletariat.

One of the obstacles in Khrushchev's path was the veneration in which Stalin's name was held among the common people, not only in the Soviet Union but all over the world. Accordingly, amidst rapturous applause from the imperialists, Khrushchev denounced Stalin. Instead of undertaking an objective analysis of past achievements and failures, with a view to drawing the correct lessons for the future, he exploited the people's natural revulsion at his disclosures of crimes committed under Stalin's leadership in order to conceal, under the pretext of combating the 'personality cult', his own calculated betrayal of Marxism-Leninism. He chose to forget that, as a member of the Party leadership himself for many years, he too was answerable for its mistakes, and that, during Stalin's lifetime, no one had been more vociferous in praising him than he had. It is true that the praise of Stalin had been carried to extremes, having been inflated by bourgeois-bureaucratic officials, who were adept at 'waving the red flag in order to destroy the red flag'; but essentially it was a spontaneous expression of popular feeling. The workers and peasants of the Soviet Union were devoted to Stalin, just as they were devoted to Lenin, because they knew that to them they owed everything.

This chapter may be concluded with the words of Mao Tse-tung:

> The Soviet Union was the first socialist state, and the Communist Party of the Soviet Union was founded by Lenin. Although the leadership of the Soviet Party has been usurped by revisionists, I would urge comrades to remain firm in the conviction that the masses of the Soviet people and of party members and cadres are good, that they desire revolution, and that revisionist rule will not last long. (PR 69-18.27.)

CHAPTER VIII

The Proletarian Cultural Revolution

> The communist revolution is the most radical rupture with traditional property relations; no wonder that its development involves the most radical rupture with traditional ideas.
>
> —*Communist Manifesto*

1. National Liberation

The proclamation of the Chinese People's Republic in October 1949 marked the victorious conclusion of a long and complex revolutionary war, including both civil war and anti-Japanese war, which began with the formation of the Chinese Red Army (now the People's Liberation Army) in 1927 and extended gradually over the whole of China. It was essentially a peasant war (MSW 2.366)—an armed struggle for the land. Peasant insurrections had been a feature of Chinese history for more than two thousand years. They were all defeated, because the peasantry as a class is incapable of leading a revolution. But this was a new kind of peasant war, in which the peasants were led by the proletariat and its vanguard, the Communist Party. Its fighting force was an army of a new type, close to the masses, organised on the principles of democratic centralism, active in production and administration as well as in fighting, providing everywhere it went a practical example of proletarian morality and self-sacrifice in the service of the people. The result was that, when liberation came in 1949, the new people's government had at its disposal a reserve of experienced cadres ready to give leadership in all the tasks of socialist construction. In addition, it received for several years valuable assistance from the Soviet Union, and it had the Soviet experience of socialist construction, both positive and negative, to learn from.

In the summer of 1949, reviewing the period of armed struggle which was then drawing to an end, Mao Tse-tung said:

> A well-disciplined Party armed with the theory of Marxism-Leninism, using the method of self-criticism and linked with the masses of the people; an army under the leadership of such a Party; a united front of all revolutionary classes and all revolutionary groups under the leadership of such a Party—these are the three main weapons with which we have defeated the enemy. . . . Relying on them, we have won basic victory. We have travelled a tortuous road. . We have struggled against opportunist deviations in our Party, both Right and 'Left'. Whenever we made serious mistakes on these three matters, the revolution suffered setbacks. Taught by mistakes and setbacks, we have become wiser and handle our affairs better. It is hard for any political party or person to avoid mistakes, but we should make as few as possible. Once a mistake is made, we should correct it, and the more quickly and thoroughly the better. (MSW 4.422.)

In order to fulfil the tasks that lay ahead, it was necessary that the Party should adapt itself to the new situation, in which the centre of the struggle had shifted from the battlefield to the farms and factories and government departments. In this situation the Party would find itself faced with a new enemy, or rather with an old enemy in a new disguise:

Very soon we shall be victorious throughout the country. This victory will breach the eastern front of imperialism and will have great international significance. To win this victory will not require much more time and effort, but to consolidate it will. The bourgeoisie doubts our ability to construct. The imperialists reckon that eventually we will beg alms from them in order to live. With victory, certain moods may grow within the Party—arrogance, the airs of a self-styled hero, inertia, and unwillingness to make progress, love of pleasure and distaste for continued hard living. With victory, the people will be grateful to us, and the bourgeoisie will come forward to flatter us. It has been proved that the enemy cannot conquer us by force of arms. However, the flattery of the bourgeoisie may conquer the weak-willed in our ranks. There may be some Communists, who were not conquered by enemies with guns and were worthy of the name of heroes for standing up to those enemies, but who cannot withstand sugar-coated bullets; they will be defeated by sugar-coated bullets. We must guard against such a situation. (MSW 4.373.)

Chairman Mao looked to the future with cautious confidence :

The Chinese revolution is great, but the road after the revolution will be longer, the work greater and more arduous. This must be made clear now in the Party. The comrades must be taught to remain modest, prudent and free from arrogance and rashness in their style of work. The comrades must be taught to preserve the style of plain living and hard struggle. We have the Marxist-Leninist weapon of criticism and self-criticism. We can get rid of a bad style and keep the good. We can learn what we did not know. We are not only good at destroying the old world, we are also good at building the new.

Not only can the Chinese people live without begging alms from the imperialists, they will live a better life than that in the imperialist countries. (MSW 4.374.)

The proclamation of the People's Republic was the outward expression of three radical changes in Chinese society.

First, the completion of the struggle for national liberation. Not only had the whole country (with the exception of Taiwan) been freed from imperialist oppression, but, for the first time in history, the national minorities, which accounted for about six per cent of the population, acquired equal rights with the Han people.

Second, the completion of the bourgeois-democratic revolution. All feudal relations were abolished. In the countryside, the land was divided among the peasantry on the principle of 'the land to the tillers'. In the towns, the capital belonging to the comprador bourgeoisie was confiscated, while the national bourgeoisie retained their ownership of the factories, subject to state control of raw materials, markets and labour conditions. At the same time a system of representative government was established, based on universal suffrage and supported by a coalition of those political parties which had taken part in the struggle for national liberation.

Third, the inception of the socialist revolution. In the countryside, the peasants were encouraged to form mutual-aid groups. These were to develop later into agricultural co-operatives and later still into communes; and, thanks to the proletarian leadership given through the peasant associations, these successive stages were carried through without serious opposition from the rich peasants. In the towns, the national bourgeoisie were encouraged to enter into agreements for joint state and private ownership. This arrangement had the advantage of securing the co-operation of former factory-owners, with their business training and administrative experience, in the socialist development of industry. And lastly, the Party initiated a series of mass movements, beginning with the San Fan movement of 1952, which was directed against graft, corruption and bureaucracy, and culminating in the proletarian cultural revolution (1966-68). These movements grew in breadth and depth, as one followed another, but their underlying purpose was the same— to carry the class struggle through to the end by calling on the masses to take the initiative : 'Dare to think ! dare to speak ! dare to act !'

2. *The Handling of Contradictions*

Are there contradictions in socialist society? If so, what is their nature and how are they to be resolved?

The answer is, in the first place, that there must be contradictions in socialist society, because there are contradictions everywhere :

Marxist philosophy holds that the law of the unity of opposites is a fundamental law of the universe. This law operates universally, whether in the natural world, in human society, or in man's thinking. Between the opposites in a contradiction there is at once unity and struggle, and it is this that impels things to move and change. Contradictions exist everywhere, but they differ in accordance with the different nature of different things. In any given phenomenon or thing, the unity of opposites is conditional, temporary and transitory, and hence relative, whereas the struggle of opposites is absolute. Lenin gave a very clear exposition of this law. In our country, a growing number of people have come to understand it. For many people, however, acceptance of this law is one thing, and its application in examining and dealing with problems is quite another. Many dare not openly admit that contradictions still exist among the people of our country, although it is these very contradictions that are pushing our society forward. Many do not admit that contradictions continue to exist in a socialist society, with the result that they are handicapped and passive when confronted with social contradictions; they do not understand that socialist society will grow more united and consolidated through the ceaseless process of the correct handling and resolving of contradictions. For this reason, we need to explain things to our people, and to our cadres in the first place, in order to help them understand the contradictions in a socialist society and learn to use correct methods for handling these contradictions. (MFE 91, cf. LCW 38.360.)

Granted the existence of contradictions in socialist society, what is their nature? They are of two kinds: contradictions among the people, which are non-antagonistic by nature, and contradictions between the people and the enemy, which are antagonistic by nature. Contradictions between the classes that support the revolution—for example, between the proletariat and the peasantry—belong to the first kind; contradictions between the classes that support the revolution, on the one hand, and the remnants of the old exploiting classes—for example, the former landlords—on the other, belong to the second kind. The distinction between these two kinds of contradiction in socialist society corresponds to the two aspects of the people's democratic dictatorship—democracy for the people and dictatorship over the reactionaries.

Thus, both non-antagonistic and antagonistic contradictions exist in socialist society. Moreover, if handled incorrectly, the non-antagonistic contradictions may become antagonistic, and conversely, if handled correctly, antagonistic contradictions may become non-antagonistic. Thus, the contradiction between the proletariat and the peasantry is non-antagonistic. Agriculture is required to produce a surplus in order to provide capital for industrial development, while it is itself dependent on industry for the machines which increase its productivity; yet, owing to the division between town and country inherited from the old society (MEG 64), agricultural labour is less productive than industrial labour. If this contradiction is not handled correctly, it will be impossible to maintain a proper balance between agricultural and industrial development, and then the contradiction between the two classes may become antagonistic. Conversely, the contradiction between the national bourgeoisie and the proletariat in the old China was antagonistic, being a contradiction between exploiters and exploited; but in the special conditions of the Chinese revolution, explained in Chapter II, this contradiction was handled in such a way as to become non-antagonistic. It had not, however, disappeared. Under the system of joint state and private ownership, the former factory owners continued for many years to receive a fixed interest on their capital. This was still a form of exploitation, though only a mitigated form. The contradiction between the proletariat and the bourgeoisie has still not been finally resolved.

For these reasons, it is vitally necessary to understand that class contradictions and class struggle continue to exist in socialist society and with them the possibility of a reversion to capitalism :

In China, although in the main socialist transformation has been completed with respect to the system of ownership, and although the large-scale and turbulent class struggles of the masses characteristic of the previous revolutionary periods have in the main come to an end, there are still remnants of the overthrown landlord and comprador classes, there is still a bourgeoisie, and the remoulding of the petty bourgeoisie has only just started. The class struggle is by no means over. The class struggle between the proletariat and the bourgeoisie, the class struggle between the different political forces, and the class struggle in the ideological field between the proletariat and the bourgeoisie will continue to be long and tortuous and at times will even become very acute. The proletariat seeks to transform the world according to its own world outlook, and so does the bourgeoisie. In this respect, the question of which will win out, socialism or capitalism, is still not really settled. (MFE 115.)

Class struggle, the struggle for production, and scientific experiment are the three great revolutionary movements for building a mighty socialist country. These movements are a sure guarantee that Communists will be free from bureaucracy and immune against revisionism and dogmatism, and will forever remain invincible. They are a reliable guarantee that the proletariat will be able to unite with the broad working masses and realise a democratic dictatorship. If, in the absence of these movements, the landlords, rich peasants, counter-revolutionaries, bad elements and ogres of all kinds were allowed to crawl out, while our cadres were to shut their eyes to all this, and in many cases fail even to differentiate between the enemy and ourselves but were to collaborate with the enemy and become corrupted and demoralised, if our cadres were thus dragged into the enemy camp or the enemy were able to sneak into our ranks, and if many of our workers, peasants and intellectuals were left defenceless against both the soft and the hard tactics of the enemy—then it would not take long, perhaps only several years or a decade, or several decades at most, before a counter-revolutionary restoration on a national scale inevitably occurred, the Marxist-Leninist Party would undoubtedly become a revisionist party or a fascist party, and the whole of China would change its colour. (MQ 40.)

Socialist society covers a fairly long historical period. In the historical period of socialism there are still classes, class contradictions and class struggle, there is the struggle between the socialist road and the capitalist road, and there is the danger of capitalist restoration. We must recognise the protracted and complex nature of this struggle. We must heighten our vigilance. We must conduct socialist education. We must correctly understand and handle class contradictions and class struggle, distinguish the contradictions between ourselves and the enemy from those among the people, and handle them correctly. Otherwise a socialist country like ours will turn into its opposite and degenerate, and a capitalist restoration will take place. (PR 69-18.15.)

3. The Capitalist Road

In 1927 Mao Tse-tung wrote :

So long as classes exist, contradictions between correct and incorrect ideas in the Communist Party are reflections within the Party of class contradictions. At first, with regard to certain issues, such contradictions may not manifest themselves as antagonistic. But with the development of the class struggle, they may grow and become antagonistic.

The history of the Communist Party of the Soviet Union shows that the contradictions between the correct thinking of Lenin and Stalin and the fallacious thinking of Trotsky, Bukharin and others did not at first manifest themselves in an antagonistic form, but that later they did develop into antagonism. There are similar cases in the history of the Chinese Communist Party.... At present, the contradiction between correct and incorrect thinking in our Party does not manifest itself in an antagonistic form, and if comrades who have committed mistakes can correct them, it will not develop into antagonism. Therefore, the Party must on the one hand wage a serious struggle against erroneous thinking, and on the other give the comrades who have committed errors ample opportunity to wake up. This being the case, excessive struggle is obviously inappropriate. But, if the people who have committed errors persist in them and aggravate them, there is the possibility that this contradiction will develop into antagonism. (MSW 1.344.)

In the cultural revolution the masses were encouraged to hold meetings in order 'to expose every kind of ghost and monster and also to criticise the shortcomings and errors in the work of the persons in charge' (PR 66-33.7). In the course of these meetings it became known that for many years there had existed within the Party leadership a faction working in opposition to Mao Tse-tung under the direction of Liu Shao-chi. This faction represented the interests of one section of the national bourgeoisie.

It was pointed out in Chapter II that in the special conditions of China the national bourgeoisie was won over to the worker-peasant alliance in the struggle against feudalism and imperialism :

In our country the contradiction between the

working class and the national bourgeoisie belongs to the category of contradictions among the people. By and large, the class struggle between the two is a class struggle within the ranks of the people, because the Chinese national bourgeoisie has a dual character. In the period of the bourgeois-democratic revolution, it had a revolutionary as well as a conciliationist side to its character. In the period of the socialist revolution, exploitation of the working class for profit constitutes one side of the character of the national bourgeoisie, while its support of the Constitution and its willingness to accept socialist transformation constitutes the other. The national bourgeoisie differs from the imperialists, the landlords, and the bureaucratic capitalists. The contradiction between the national bourgeoisie and the working class is one between the exploiter and the exploited, and is therefore antagonistic in nature. But in the concrete conditions of China this antagonistic class contradiction can, if properly handled, be transformed into a non-antagonistic one and be resolved by peaceful methods. However, it can change into a contradiction between ourselves and the enemy, if we do not handle it properly and do not follow the policy of uniting with, criticising and educating the national bourgeoisie, or if the national bourgeoisie does not accept this policy of ours. (MFE 82.)

Thanks to the correct handling of this contradiction most members of the national bourgeoisie gave their support to the people's democratic dictatorship; but some of them, who wanted a capitalist China, resisted the further advance of the revolution and so aligned themselves with the counter-revolutionary forces. It was this section of the national bourgeoisie whose interests were served, within the Party leadership, by Liu Shao-chi. His opposition to Mao Tse-tung expressed the contradiction between the pro-capitalist elements and the proletariat, which had been present from the beginning but became intensified after 1945, when the war against Japan ended, and still more after 1949, when the bourgeois-democratic revolution passed into the socialist revolution.

The line pursued by Liu Shao-chi was consistently opportunist in content, though presented sometimes in a rightist and sometimes in a leftist form. The difference in form was dictated by tactical considerations, being designed to exploit the vacillation characteristic of bourgeois and petty-bourgeois ideology. When the Party was debating whether to advance or retreat, Liu Shao-chi was in favour of retreat; when the Party had decided to advance, Liu Shao-chi was in favour of advancing so rapidly as to risk defeat. The development of this initially non-antagonistic contradiction may be seen from the stand which he took on successive issues in the post-war period.

At the end of the second world war, the Communist Parties of the liberated countries found themselves in a stronger position than ever before. Through their leadership of the resistance they had won the support of the masses, whereas the bourgeoisie was divided and discredited. They were faced, therefore, with a choice—either to lead the people forward to the socialist revolution or to hand in their arms and help the bourgeoisie to re-establish the old order, which had been shaken to its foundations by the war. It was, in effect, a choice between the socialist road and the capitalist road. The Parties of Western Europe chose the latter. In China, too, this road was recommended by some of the Party leaders, including Liu Shao-chi. It would have meant entering a coalition with the Kuomintang on terms which would have placed the revolutionary armies under their control. Thanks to the leadership of Mao Tse-tung, the Chinese Communists decided to fight on.

The land reform was planned by the Party with the aim of abolishing feudal relations in the countryside. After making a careful assessment of the properties belonging to the landlords and rich peasants, the peasant associations were to take over their surplus land and redistribute it among the poor peasants. This line was for some time distorted by Liu Shao-chi, who encouraged the poor peasants to believe that the purpose of the redistribution was to give middle-peasant status to them all. At the existing level of agricultural production this was impossible, and the land reform movement would have ended in failure, if the line had not been corrected by Mao Tse-tung (MSW 4.197).

After the abolition of feudal relations, the question arose, what was to be the next stage? Was agriculture to develop on a socialist or a capitalist basis? The Party line was, still relying on the poor peasants, to advance through mutual-aid groups to the formation of co-operatives and so to collectivisation. The agricultural surplus was to provide a basis for building up heavy industry, but part of it was to be invested in light industry, which would both create a demand for industrial crops and supply a sufficient quantity of consumer goods to ensure that an undue strain was not placed on the peasantry. This line was opposed by Liu Shao-chi, who argued as follows. Collectivisation was impossible without machines and must therefore wait on industrial development. In the meantime agriculture was to be developed on capitalist lines by permitting the buying and selling of land and the employment of wage-labour. 'It will be time enough to talk about collectivisation', he said, 'when seventy per cent of the peasants have become rich peasants.' It will be seen that this line resembles the line put forward in the Soviet Union by

Bukharin, who argued that, given a free market in agriculture, the kulaks would 'grow into socialism'.

When the co-operative movement was gathering speed in the mid-fifties, Liu Shao-chi began by attempting to slow it down. Later, after it had gone ahead in spite of him, he advocated an extreme form of equalitarianism, just as he had done in the land reform. Later still, when the movement was in difficulties after a run of bad harvests, he was again advocating a free market and freedom of private enterprise. When the Party was calling on the workers to 'fight self and criticise revisionism'—that is, to oppose, in themselves and others, all forms of bourgeois individualism and self-interest—Liu Shao-chi was advocating 'self-cultivation' and the use of material incentives.

It is clear, therefore, that from the beginning there had been a conflict within the Party leadership between these two lines—the proletarian line, represented by Mao Tse-tung, and the bourgeois line, represented by Liu Shao-chi. The bourgeois line deviated now to the right and now to the 'left', but always in opposition to the proletarian line.

Encouraged by the example of Khrushchev and the new revisionists in the Soviet Union, Liu Shao-chi and his faction made plans for a similar take-over in China. Their number was not large, but they held some key positions in the Party leadership, through which they were able to exert widespread influence, misleading and confusing the rank-and-file. The issue came to a head in the spring of 1966. On May 16 a circular, drafted by Mao Tse-tung, was sent out by the Central Committee to all Party members. In this document it was stated :

There are a number of these representatives of the bourgeoisie in the Central Committee and in the Party, government and other departments at the central as well as the provincial, municipal, and autonomous-region level.

The whole Party must hold high the great banner of the proletarian cultural revolution, thoroughly expose the reactionary bourgeois stand of those so-called 'academic authorities' who oppose the Party and socialism, thoroughly criticise and repudiate the reactionary bourgeois ideas in the sphere of academic work, education, journalism, literature and art publishing, and seize the leadership in these cultural spheres. To achieve this, it is necessary at the same time to criticise and repudiate those representatives of the bourgeoisie who have sneaked into the Party, the government, the army and all spheres of culture, to clear them out or transfer some of them to other positions.

Those representatives of the bourgeoisie who have sneaked into the Party, the government, the army, and various cultural circles are a bunch of counter-revolutionary revisionists. Once conditions are ripe, they will seize political power and turn the dictatorship of the proletariat into a dictatorship of the bourgeoisie. Some of them we have already seen through, others we have not. Some are still trusted by us and are being trained as our successors, persons like Khrushchev, for example, who are still nestling beside us. Party committees at all levels must pay full attention to this matter. (PR 67-21.10.)

In this way the Party was alerted to the danger, and it responded by calling on the masses to criticise its work without constraint in order to identify and isolate the enemy :

As Chairman Mao pointed out in his talk in February 1967 : 'In the past we have waged struggles in rural areas, in factories, in the cultural field, and we carried out the socialist education

156

movement. But all this failed to solve the problem, because we did not find a form, a method, to arouse the broad masses to expose our dark aspect openly, in an all-round way, and from below'.

Now we have found this form—it is the great proletarian cultural revolution. It is only by arousing the masses in their hundreds of millions to air their views freely, write big-character posters, and hold great debates, that the renegades, enemy agents, and capitalist-roaders in power, who have wormed their way into the Party, can be exposed and their plots to restore capitalism smashed. (PR 69-18.16.)

4. *Mass Participation in Government*

When Lenin called for a 'cultural revolution', he realised that for the complete victory of socialism it was necessary that the masses of the workers and peasants should take the work of government into their own hands, and that to achieve this they must raise their cultural level to the point at which they could impose their own proletarian ideology in place of the old bourgeois ideology and so clear away the bureaucratic obstacles behind which the bourgeoisie had entrenched themselves.

These, too, were the aims of the Chinese cultural revolution. It was designed, not merely to eliminate the elements hostile to socialism, but to enable the working class to 'exercise leadership in everything', to 'place politics in command of administration', and to ensure that everyone serving as an official should 'remain one of the common people'.

In order to achieve these aims it was necessary to launch an all-out offensive against bourgeois ideology in such a way that the masses would be actively involved :

Although the bourgeoisie has been overthrown, it

is still trying to use the old ideas, culture, customs and habits of the exploiting classes to corrupt the masses, capture their minds, and endeavour to stage a come-back. The proletariat must do just the opposite. It must meet head-on every challenge of the bourgeoisie in the ideological field and use the new ideas, culture, customs and habits of the proletariat to change the mental outlook of the whole of society. (PR 66-33.6.)

In the great proletarian cultural revolution, the only method is for the masses to liberate themselves, and any method of doing things on their behalf must not be used.

Trust the masses, rely on them, and respect their initiative. Cast out fear. Don't be afraid of disorder.... Let the masses educate themselves in this great revolutionary movement and learn to distinguish between right and wrong and between correct and incorrect ways of doing things. (PR 66-33.7.)

Such was the 'socialist offensive' against the 'survivals of capitalism in people's minds', for which Stalin had called in the Soviet Union; but there, being less close to the masses, the Party was not strong enough to draw them into the struggle.

During the cultural revolution there sprang up a new organisational unit—the revolutionary committee. It is based on the 'three-in-one' combination: that is, its members, who are elected, subject to recall, and directly responsible to the people, are drawn from the Party, the People's Liberation Army, and the mass organisations. These committees are a creation of the masses. They have sprung up at all levels, from the factory or commune to the organs of provincial and regional government, and their function is to provide the link through which the masses can participate directly in the running of the country :

This three-in-one organ of power enables our proletarian political power to strike deep roots among the masses. Chairman Mao points out : 'The most fundamental principle in the reform of state organs is that they must keep in contact with the masses'. The representatives of the revolutionary masses, particularly the representatives of the working people—the workers and peasants—who have come forward *en masse* in the course of the great proletarian cultural revolution, are revolutionary fighters with practical experience. Representing the interests of the revolutionary masses, they participate in the leading groups at various levels. This provides revolutionary committees at these levels with a broad mass foundation. Direct participation by the revolutionary masses in the running of the country and the enforcement of revolutionary supervision from below over the organs of political power at various levels play a very important role in ensuring that our leading groups at all levels always adhere to the mass line, maintain the closest relations with the masses, represent their interests at all times, and serve the people heart and soul. (PR 68-14.6.)

The formation of these revolutionary committees marks an important advance in the socialist revolution. The masses have begun to take over directly the running of the country. When this process is complete, the transition to communism will have begun; but it is a lengthy process, and its successful completion can only be ensured by continuing the class struggle to the end. As Chairman Mao has said :

We have won a great victory. But the defeated class will still struggle. These people are still around, and this class still exists. Therefore we cannot speak of final victory. Not even for decades. We must not lose our vigilance. According to the Leninist viewpoint, the final victory of a socialist country requires not only the efforts of the proletariat and the broad masses of the people at home, but also involves the victory of the world revolution and the abolition of the system of exploitation of man by man on the whole globe, upon which all mankind will be emancipated. Therefore, it is wrong to speak lightly of the final victory of the revolution in our country : it runs counter to Leninism and does not conform to facts. (PR 69-18.23.)

5. *Revolution and Production*

Summing up the economic results of the cultural revolution, Lin Piao said :

Our country has seen good harvests in agricultural production for years running, and there is also a thriving situation in industrial production and in science and technology. The enthusiasm of the broad masses of the working people in both revolution and production has soared to unprecedented heights. Many factories, mines and other enterprises have time and again topped their production records, creating all-time highs in production. The technical revolution is making constant progress. The market is flourishing and prices are stable. By the end of 1968 we had redeemed all the national bonds. Our country is now a socialist country with neither internal nor external debts. (PR 69-18.22.)

He went on to explain the principle of 'grasp revolution, promote production', which had become one of the key slogans of the revolution :

'Grasp revolution, promote production'—this principle is absolutely correct. It correctly explains the relationship between revolution and production, between consciousness and matter, between the superstructure and the economic basis, and between the relations of production and the productive forces. Chairman Mao always teaches us : 'Political work is the life-blood of all economic work.' Lenin denounced the opportunists who were opposed to approaching problems politically. 'Politics cannot but have precedence over economics. To argue differently means forgetting the ABC of Marxism' (LCW 32.83). ... Politics is the concentrated expression of economics. If we fail to make revolution in the superstructure, fail to arouse the broad masses of the workers and peasants, fail to criticise the revisionist line, fail to expose the handful of renegades, enemy agents, capitalist-roaders in power and counter-revolutionaries, and fail to consolidate the leadership of the proletariat, how can we further consolidate the socialist economic base and further develop the socialist productive forces? This is not to replace production by revolution, but to use revolution to command production, promote it and lead it forward. (PR 69-18.22.)

This concept of the relation between revolution and production as a unity of opposites is an expression of what Lenin called 'revolutionary dialectics' (LCW 33.476, cf. 25.422). It is deeply rooted in the thought of Mao Tse-tung, going back to the rectification movements of the pre-liberation period (MSW 3.328), and it rests on one of the fundamental principles of dialectical and historical materialism. Marx wrote :

In the social production of their life, men enter into definite relations that are indispensable and independent of their will, relations of production which correspond to a definite stage of development of their material productive forces. The sum total of these relations of production constitutes the economic structure of society, the real foundation, on which rises a legal and political superstructure and to which correspond definite forms of social consciousness. It is not the consciousness of men that determines their being, but, on the contrary, it is their social being that determines their consciousness. (ME 1.362.)

At the same time, while determined by the economic basis, the superstructure reacts upon it :

Political, juridical, philosophical, religious, literary, artistic etc. development is based on economic development. But all these react upon one another and also upon the economic basis. It is not that the economic condition is the *cause* and *alone active,* while everything else is only a passive effect. There is, rather, interaction on the basis of economic necessity, which *ultimately* always asserts itself. (ME 2.504.)

It follows that in certain conditions, and especially in revolutionary situations, the consciousness of men, having comprehended the laws governing their social being, may become the decisive factor. Mao Tse-tung writes :

True, the productive forces, practice, and the economic base generally play the principal and decisive role : whoever denies this is not a materialist. But it must also be admitted that in certain conditions such aspects as the relations of production, theory, and the superstructure in turn manifest themselves in the principal and decisive role. When it is impossible for the productive forces to develop without a change in the relations of production, then the change in the relations of production plays the principal and decisive role. The creation and advocacy of revolutionary theory plays the principal and decisive role in those times of which Lenin said, 'Without revolutionary theory there can be no revolutionary movement' (LCW 5.369). When a task, no matter what, has to be performed, but there is as yet no guiding line, method, plan or policy, the principal and decisive thing is to decide on a guiding line, method, plan or policy. When the superstructure (politics, culture, etc.) obstructs the development of the economic base, political and cultural changes become principal and decisive. Are we going against materialism when we say this? No. The reason is that, while we recognise that in the general development of history the material determines the mental and social being determines social consciousness, we also—and indeed must—recognise the reaction of mental on material things, of social consciousness on social being, and of the superstructure on the economic base. This does not go against materialism; on the contrary, it avoids mechanical materialism and firmly upholds dialectical materialism. (MSW 1.336.)

If, while determined ultimately by the economic basis, the political and ideological superstructure reacts upon it, and at times decisively, it follows that in its work of socialist construction the proletariat must maintain and extend its dictatorship simultaneously in both basis and superstructure. In the Soviet Union, owing to the pressure of capitalist encirclement, which forced the pace of internal development, this problem was not solved; but the solution has been found in China, thanks to the lead given by Mao Tse-tung :

The new social system has only just been established and requires time for its consolidation. It must not be assumed that the new system can be completely consolidated the moment it is established, for that is impossible. It has to be consolidated step by step. To achieve its ultimate consolidation, it is necessary not only to bring about the socialist industrialisation of the country and persevere in the socialist revolution on the economic front, but to carry on constant and arduous socialist revolutionary struggles and socialist education on the political and ideological fronts. Moreover, various contributory international factors are required. (MQ 27.)

6. *Communist Labour*

Let us return to the subbotniks. The first of these, held in the spring of 1919, were, as Lenin said, only a beginning. On May 1, 1920, an All-Russia subbotnik was held, in which 450,000 workers were involved in the city of Moscow alone. A leaflet was circulated with a message from Lenin, in which he said :

Let us build a new society!

We were not daunted by defeats during the great revolutionary war against Tsarism, against the bourgeoisie, against the omnipotent imperialist world powers.

We shall not be daunted by the gigantic difficulties and the errors that are inevitable at the outset of a most difficult task : the transformation of all labour habits and customs requires decades. . . . We shall work to do away with the accursed maxim, 'Every man for himself and the devil take the hindmost', the habit of looking on work merely as a duty and of considering rightful only that work which is paid for at certain rates. We shall work to inculcate into the people's minds, to form into a habit, and bring into the everyday life of the masses, the rule 'All for each and each for all', the rule 'From each according to his ability, to each according to his needs'; we shall work for the gradual but steady introduction of communist discipline and communist labour.

We have shifted a huge mountain, a huge mass of conservatism, ignorance, stubborn adherence to the habits of 'free trade' and the 'free' buying and selling of human labour-power like any other commodity. We have begun to undermine and destroy the firmest, age-long and ingrained habits. In a single year our subbotniks have made an immense stride forward. They are still infinitely weak, but that will not daunt us. We have seen our 'infinitely weak' Soviet state, before our own eyes, gaining strength and becoming a mighty world force as a result of our own efforts. We shall work for years and decades practising subbotniks, developing them, spreading them, improving them, converting them into a habit. We shall achieve the victory of communist labour. (LCW 31.124.)

It is the same message that has been conveyed to the Chinese people by Mao Tse-tung. Led by the Communist Party, the masses of workers and peasants throw off the burden of imperialism and feudalism, and there is released within them, freed at last from exploitation, an inexhaustible store of creative energy, which enables them to transform the world. In June 1945, addressing the Seventh Party Congress, he recalled the following folk-tale :

There is an ancient Chinese fable called 'The Foolish Old Man who Removed the Mountains'. It tells of an old man who lived in northern China long, long ago and was known as the Foolish Old Man of North Mountain. His house faced south and beyond his doorway stood the two great peaks, Taihang and Wangwu, obstructing the way. He called his sons, and hoe in hand they began to dig up these mountains with great determination. Another greybeard, known as the Wise Old Man, saw them and said derisively, 'How silly of you to do this! It is quite impossible for you few to dig up these huge mountains.' The Foolish Old Man replied, 'When I die, my sons will carry on; when they die, there will be my grandsons, and so on to infinity. High as they are, the mountains cannot grow any higher, and with every bit we dig they will be that much lower. Why can't we clear them away?' Having refuted the Wise Old Man's wrong view, he went on digging every day, unshaken in his conviction. God was moved by this, and sent down two angels, who carried the mountains away on their backs.

Today, two big mountains lie like a dead weight on the Chinese people. One is imperialism, the other is feudalism. The Chinese Communist Party has long made up its mind to dig them up. We must persevere and work unceasingly, and we too will touch God's heart. Our God is none other than the masses of the Chinese people. If they stand up and dig together with us, why can't these two mountains be cleared away? (MSW 3.321.)

Four years later, on the eve of the proclamation of the People's Republic, he said:

Of all things in the world, people are the most precious. Under the leadership of the Communist Party, so long as there are people, every kind of miracle can be performed.... We believe that revolution can change everything, and that before long there will arise a new China with a big population and a great wealth of products, where life will be abundant and culture will flourish. All pessimistic views are utterly groundless. (MSW 4.454.)

Revolution can change everything. The proletarian cultural revolution is a mass movement, without precedent in history, for remoulding both man and nature. In this movement, following the road of the October Revolution, the Chinese workers and peasants have given an example to the world, showing the workers and peasants of all countries that through revolution poverty can be transformed into plenty. And the key to the success of the movement lies in the relation between the Party and the masses. Having boundless confidence in the masses, the Party calls on them to exercise their initiative more and more boldly, and the masses respond.

In 1955, during the socialist upsurge in the countryside, which led to the creation of the people's communes, Mao Tse-tung wrote:

> The masses have boundless creative power. They can organise themselves and concentrate on places and branches of work where they can give full play to their energy; they can concentrate on production in breadth and depth and create more and more undertakings for their own well-being. (MQ 118.)

Since then considerable progress has been made in the mechanisation of agriculture, and it will not be long before the Chinese workers and peasants are equipped with all the advanced techniques of modern society. In the meantime, however, rather than wait for machines, they are prepared to work with the same implements that their ancestors used for thousands of years, but to work in a new way. On December 9, 1970—only a few weeks after the flood disaster in East Bengal, in which over a quarter of a million peasants lost their lives—a French newspaper correspondent sent the following despatch from Peking:

> A mere twelve miles from Peking 100,000 Chinese are working steadily round the clock, in spite of the bitter cold, to change the course of a river. Their only

tools are wheelbarrows, shovels, pick-axes, and the thoughts of Mao Tse-tung.

Diplomats in Peking who take the highway to the airport south-east of the capital invariably slow their cars when they cross the bridge over the Wen Yu River to gaze with astonishment at the human ant-heap that forms a dark patch, dotted with innumerable red flags, stretching to the horizon.

The picture is even more striking in the light of dawn, and one might be tempted to classify it as one of those stereotypes of the Chinese reality intended for foreigners.

According to officials, the Wen Yu development scheme is only part of a scheme for the whole of the Hai River in north-east China. The Hai has a history of floods and droughts.

According to the Chinese press, hundreds of thousands of peasants answered Chairman Mao's call in 1963 to 'tame' the Hai. Since then enough earth has been shifted to build a dyke 3 feet high and 3 feet wide stretching 37 times round the globe.

Drainage works and the building of 900 miles of dykes for 19 main tributaries of the Hai River have meant that at the river's principal outflow point, Tsientsin, the discharge has risen from 1,000 cubic yards a second to 13,000 cubic yards. This has spared 8,250,000 acres of arable land from the danger of floods.

At the end of October the authorities mobilised Hopei-province peasants, soldiers, militia, and Peking citizens to work on 34 miles of the Wen Yu, a tributary of the Hai. The job should have taken four months, but the authorities say it is already four-fifths completed.

Recently I visited two of the work sites. There was no noise of machinery, just the heavy breathing of men swinging pick-axes, the neighing of ponies, the shouts of cart drivers, the slogans chanted by the workers, and the revolutionary music played over the loud-speakers.

To dig into the river bed it is necessary to break ice. Yet I saw one man, aged about sixty, stripped to the waist so that he could swing his pick-axe better.

Day and night, in eight-hour shifts, and sometimes in sub-zero temperatures, relay teams deepen the river bed, construct dikes, and eliminate various tributaries to give the river a new bed.

For the workers all methods are valid for responding to Chairman Mao's appeal. They may uproot a tree-trunk by the sheer weight of their bodies.

They live in huts or enormous tents surrounded by small walls of earth and straw to keep out the icy wind. Food is brought to the site in great steaming pots. (*The Times* 70-12-10.)

As Marx said, 'When theory grips the masses, it becomes a material force' (MER 50).

Let me conclude with one more quotation from Chairman Mao :

The masses are the real heroes, while we ourselves are often childish and ignorant, and without this understanding it is impossible to acquire even the most rudimentary knowledge. (MSW 3.12.)

References

Marx and Engels

ME. Marx and Engels, Selected works in two volumes. Moscow, 1955.

ME 1.21–65. The Communist Manifesto. February 1848.

ME 1.106–17. Address of the Central Committee to the Communist League. March 1850.

ME. 1.319–242. Marx. The class struggles in France 1848–1850. 1850.

ME. 1.361–65. Marx, A contribution to the critique of political economy. January 1859.

ME 1.473–85. Marx, The civil war in France: introduction by Engels. March 1891.

ME 2.16–48. Marx, Critique of the Gotha Programme. May 1875.

ME 2.49–61. Engels, On social relations in Russia. April 1875.

ME 2.452. Marx, Letter to Joseph Weydemeyer. March 5, 1852.

ME 2.504–06. Engels, Letter to H. Starkenburg. January 25, 1894.

MEG. Marx and Engels. The German ideology. (London, 1965) 1846.

MEP. Engels, The peasant war in Germany. (London, 1927) 1850.

MER. Marx and Engels, On religion. Moscow, 1957.

MER 41–58. Marx, A contribution to the critique of Hegel's philosophy of right. 1844.

LCW. V. I. Lenin, Collected works, 45 vols. Moscow, 1960-70.

LCW 1.335–507. The economic content of Narodism and the criticism of it in Mr. Struve's book. 1895.

LCW 2.93–121. Draft and explanation of a programme for the Social-Democratic Party. 1895–96.

LCW 3.29–607. The development of capitalism in Russia. 1899.

LCW 4.420–28. The workers' party and the peasantry. April 1901.

LCW 5.327–28. Notes on anarchism and socialism. 1901.

LCW 5.347–529. What is to be done? February 1902.

LCW 6.186–207. Revolutionary adventurism. October 1902.

LCW 6.361–432. To the rural poor. March 1903.

LCW 6.454–63. The national question in our programme. July 1903.

LCW 7.203–425. One step forward, two steps back. May 1904.

LCW 8.17–28. The autocracy and the proletariat. January 1905.

LCW 8.231–36. The proletariat and the peasantry. March 1905.

LCW 8.257–59. A revolution of the 1789 or the 1848 type? April 1905.

LCW 8.293–303. The revolutionary-democratic dictatorship of the proletariat and the peasantry. March 1905.

LCW 8.537–43. The struggle of the proletariat, senility of the bourgeoisie. June 1905.

LCW 9.13–140. Two tactics of social-democracy in the democratic revolution. July 1905.

LCW 9.230–39. Social-democracy's attitude towards the peasant movement. September 1905.

LCW 9.411–12. The aggravation of the situation in Russia. October 1905.

LCW 9.427–34. The first victory of the revolution. November 1905.

LCW 10.91–92. The stages, the trend, and the prospects of the revolution. 1905–06.

LCW 10.199–279. The victory of the Cadets and the task of the workers' party. March 1906.

LCW 10.277–309. The Unity Congress of the R.S.D.L.P. April 1906.

LCW 10.317–82. Report on the Unity Congress of the R.S.D.L.P. May 1906.

LCW 10.392–95. The Congress summed up. May 1906.

LCW 10.436–39. The land question and the fight for freedom. June 1906.

LCW 11.320–23. Party discipline and the fight against the pro-Cadet social-democrats. November 1906.

LCW 11.341–64. The crisis of Menshevism. December 1906.

LCW 11.389–95. The political situation and the tasks of the working class. December 1906.

LCW 12.104–12. Preface to the Russian translation of Karl Marx's letters to Dr Kugelmann. February 1907.

LCW 12.133–44. Draft resolutions for the Fifth Congress of the R.S.D.L.P. March 1907.

LCW 12.333–36. The agrarian question and the forces of the revolution. April 1907.

LCW 12.359–70. Preface to the Russian translation of Letters to Friedrich Sorge and others. April 1907.

LCW 12.437–88. Fifth Congress of the R.S.D.L.P. May 1907.

LCW 12.490–509. The attitude to bourgeois parties. 1907.

LCW 13.75–81. The international socialistic congress in Stuttgart. September 1907.

LCW 13.217–429. The agrarian programme of social-democracy in the first Russian revolution. December 1907.

LCW 13.432–38. The debate on the extension of the Duma's budgetary powers. February 1908.

LCW 13.440–46. Political notes. February 1908.

LCW 15.29–39. Marxism and revisionism. April 1908.

LCW 15.50–62. The assessment of the Russian revolution. April 1908.

LCW 15.383–94. A caricature of Bolshevism. April 1909.

LCW 16.296–304. The lessons of the revolution. November 1910.

LCW 16.347–52. Differences in the European labour movement. December 1910.

LCW 16.355–58. The beginning of demonstrations. December 1910.

LCW 16.359–60. What is happening in the countryside? December 1910.

LCW 16. 374–92. Inner-party struggle in Russia. 1910-11.

LCW 17.119–28. The 'peasant reform' and the proletarian-peasant revolution. March 1911.

LCW 17.139–43. In memory of the Commune. April 1911.

LCW 18.36–43. The Trudoviks and the worker democrats. May 1912.

LCW 18.143–49. A comparison of the Stolypin and the Narodnik agrarian programmes. July 1912.

LCW 19.91–92. The working class and the national question. May 1913.

LCW 19.147–69. Controversial issues: an open party and the Marxists. June 1913.

LCW 19.180–96. The question of the (general) agrarian policy of the present Government. June 1913.

LCW 19.243–51. Theses on the national question. June 1913.

LCW 19.295–301. August Bebel. August 1913.

LCW 19.354–57. Liberals and democrats on the language question. September 1913.

LCW 19.394–416. How Vera Zasulich demolishes liquidation-ism. September 1913.

LCW 19.417–31. Resolutions of the Summer (1913) Joint Conference of the C.C. of the R.S.D.L.P. and Party officials. September 1913.

LCW 19.454–57. Capitalism and workers' immigration. October 1913.

LCW 19.499–502. Letter to S.G. Shahumyan. December 6, 1913.

LCW 19.503–07. 'Cultural-national' autonomy. November 1913.

LCW 19.531–33. The nationality of pupils in Russian schools. December 1913.

LCW 19.539–45. The national programme of the R.S.D.L.P December 1913.

LCW 20.17–51. Critical remarks on the national question. December 1913.

LCW 20. 212–16. The Left Narodniks whitewash the bourgeoise. April 1914.

LCW 20.245–53. From the history of the workers' press in Russia. April 1914.

LCW 20.265–73. Concluding remarks to the symposium 'Marxism and liquidationism'. April 1914.

LCW 20.325–47. Disruption of unity under cover of outcries for unity. May 1914.

LCW 20.375–77. The agrarian question in Russia. June 1914.

LCW 20.393–454. The right of nations to self-determination. May 1914.

LCW 21.205–59. The collapse of the Second International. June 1915.

LCW 21.295–338. Socialism and war. August 1915.

LCW 21.339–43. On the slogan for a United States of Europe. August 1915.

LCW 21.407–14. The revolutionary proletariat and the right of nations to self-determination. October 1915.

LCW 21.415–20. On the two lines in the revolution. November 1915.

LCW 22.13–102. New data on the laws governing the development of capitalism in agriculture. 1915.

LCW 22.187–304. Imperialism, the highest stage of capitalism. April 1917.

LCW 22.320–60. The discussion on self-determination summed up. July 1916.

LCW 23.28–76. A caricature of Marxism and imperialist economism. October 1916.

LCW 23.77–87. The military programme of the proletarian revolution. September 1916.

LCW 23.271–77. Statistics and sociology. January 1917.

LCW 24.20–26. The tasks of the proletariat in the present revolution. April 1917.

LCW 24.38–41. The dual power. April 1917.

LCW 24.140–47. Report to the Petrograd City Conference of the R.S.D.L.P. (Bolsheviks). April 1917.

LCW 24.456–79. Materials relating to the revision of the Party programme. May 1917.

LCW 25.15–42. First All-Russian Congress of Soviets. June 1917.

LCW 25.319–65. The impending catastrophe and how to combat it. October 1917.

LCW 25.366–79. One of the fundamental questions of the revolution. September 1917.

LCW 25.381–492. The state and revolution. 1918.

LCW 26.87–136. Can the Bolsheviks retain state power? October 1917.

LCW 26.149–78. Revision of the Party programme. October 1917.

LCW 26.223–27. Letter to the Central Committee of the R.S.D.L.P.(B.). November 1, 1917.

LCW 26.453–82. Third All-Russia Congress of Soviets. January 1918.

LCW 27.68–75. Strange and monstrous. March 1918.

LCW 27.85–158. Extraordinary Seventh Congress of the R.C.P.(B.). March 1918.

LCW 27.169–201. Extraordinary Fourth All-Russia Congress of Soviets. March 1918.

LCW 27.235–77. The immediate tasks of the Soviet Government. April 1918.

LCW 27.365–81. Report on foreign policy. May 1918.

LCW 28.54–58. Comrade workers, forward to the last, decisive fight! August 1918.

LCW 28.105–13. The proletarian revolution and the renegade Kautsky. October 1918.

LCW 28.135–64. Extraordinary Sixth Congress of Soviets. November 1918.

LCW 28.185–94. The valuable admissions of Pitirim Sorokin. November 1918.

LCW 28.227–325. The proletarian revolution and the renegade Kautsky. 1918.

LCW 28.391–404. Speech at a joint session of the All-Russian Central Executive Committee, the Moscow Soviet, and All Russian Trade Union Congress. January 1919.

LCW 28.453–77. First Congress of the Communist International. March 1919.

LCW 29.19–37. Session of the Petrograd Soviet. March 1919.

LCW 29.97–140. Draft programme of the R.C.P.(B.). March 1919.

LCW 29.141–225. Eighth Congress of the R.C.P.(B.). March 1919.

LCW 29.305–13. The Third International and its place in history. April 1919.

LCW 29.333–76. The First All-Russian Congress on Adult Education. May 1919.

LCW 29.387–91. Greetings to the Hungarian workers. May 1919.

LCW 29.409–34. A great beginning. July 1919.

LCW 29.494–512. The tasks of the Third International. July 1919.

LCW 30.93–104. The dictatorship of the proletariat. October 1919.

LCW 30.107–26. Economics and politics. November 1919.

LCW 30.151–66. Address to the Second All-Russia Congress of Communist Organisations of the Peoples of the East. November 1919.

LCW 30.205–52. Seventh All-Russia Congress of Soviets. December 1919.

LCW 30.253–75. The Constituent Assembly elections and the dictatorship of the proletariat. December 1919.

LCW 30.380–402. Speech delivered at the First All-Russia Congress of Working Cossacks. March 1920.

LCW 30.417–25. Speech at a meeting of the Moscow Soviet. March 1920.

LCW 31.17–118. 'Left-wing' communism—an infantile disorder. May 1920.

LCW 31.123–25. From the first subbotnik to the All-Russia May Day subbotnik. May 1920.

LCW 31.184–201. Theses on the fundamental tasks of the Communist International. July 1920.

LCW 31.206–11. The terms of admission to the Communist International. July 1920.

LCW 31.213–63. Second Congress of the Communist International. July 1920.

LCW 31.397–402. Speech at a joint meeting of the Moscow Soviet. November 1920.

LCW 31.408–26. Our foreign and domestic position and the tasks of the Party. November 1920.

LCW 31.430–33. Speech delivered at a meeting of cell secretaries. . . . November 1920.

LCW 31.434–36. Speech delivered at a general meeting of Communists of Zamoskvorechye District, Moscow. November 1920.

LCW 31.461–533. The Eighth All-Russia Congress of Soviets. December 1920.

LCW 36.591–97. Letter to the Congress. December 1922.

LCW 36.605–11. The question of nationalities or 'autono-misation'. December 1922.

LCW 37.281–82. Letter to his mother. January 9, 1899.

LCW 38.85–243. Conspectus of Hegel's book, The science of logic. December 1914.

LCW 38.355–64. On the question of dialectics. 1914.

Stalin

SCW. J. V. Stalin, Works. 13 vols. (uncompleted). Moscow, 1952–55.

SCW 6.3–46. Thirteenth Conference of the R.C..P.(B.). January 1924.

SCW 6.71–196. The foundations of Leninism. May 1924.

SCW 6.197–245. Thirteenth Congress of the R.C.P.(B.). May 1924.

SCW 6.375–437. The October Revolution and the tactics of the Russian Communists. December 1924.

SCW 7.19–24. Dymovka. January 1925.

SCW 7.25–33. Concerning the question of the proletariat and the peasantry. January 1925.

SCW 7.135–154. The political tasks of the University of the Peoples of the East. May 1925.

SCW 7.157–214. Questions and answers. June 1925.

SCW 7.237–39. Letter to Comrade Yermakovsky. September 15, 1925.

SCW 7.265–403. The Fourteenth Congress of the C.P.S.U.(B.). December 1925.

SCW 8.13–96. Concerning questions of Leninism. January 1926.

SCW 8.245–310. The social-democratic deviation in our Party. November 1926.

SCW 9.1–155. The Seventh Enlarged Plenum of the E.C.C.I. December 1926.

SCW 10.244–55. The international character of the October Revolution. November 1927.

SCW 10.275–382. The Fifteenth Congress of the C.P.S.U.(B.). December 1927.

SCW 11.30–68. The work of the April Joint Plenum of the

Central Committee and the Central Control Commission. April 1928.

SCW 11.70–82. Speech delivered at the Eighth Congress of the All-Union Leninist Young Communist League. May 1928.

SCW 11.85–101. On the grain front. February 1928.

SCW 11.133–44. Against vulgarising the slogan of self-criticism. June 1928.

SCW 11.145–205. Plenum of the C.C., C.P.S.U.(B.). July 1928.

SCW 11.231–48. The Right danger in the C.P.S.U.(B.). October 1928.

SCW 12.242–385. Political report of the Central Committee to the Sixteenth Congress of the C.P.S.U.(B.). June 1930.

SCW 13.31–44. The tasks of business executives. February 1931.

SCW 13.160. The fifteenth anniversary of the O.G.P.U. December 1932.

SCW 13.163–219. The results of the first five-year plan. January 1933.

SCW 13.288–388. Report to the Seventeenth Party Congress. January 1934.

SL. Joseph Stalin, Leninism. London, 1940

SL. 561–90. On the draft constitution of the U.S.S.R. November 1936.

SL. 591–618. Dialectical and historical materialism. September 1938.

SL. 619–67. Report to the Eighteenth Congress of the C.P.S.U.(B.). March 1939.

SMT. The Moscow trial (January 1937) and two speeches by J. Stalin. Compiled by W. P. and Z. K. Coates. London, 1937.

SMT 249–81. Speech at the Plenum of the Central Committee of the C.P.S.U.(B.). March 3, 1937.

SP. J. Stalin, Economic problems of socialism in the U.S.S.R. Moscow, 1952.

MSW. Selected works of Mao Tse-tung. 4 vols. Peking, 1961–65.

MSW 1.13–21. Analysis of the classes in Chinese society. March 1926.

MSW 1.63–72. Why is it that red political power can exist in China? October 1928.

MSW 1.117–28. A single spark can start a prairie fire. January 1930.

MSW 1.147–52. Be concerned with the well-being of the masses, pay attention to methods of work. January 1934.

MSW 1. 179–254. Problems of strategy in China's revolutionary war. December 1936.

MSW 1.285–94. Win the masses in their millions for the anti-Japanese united national front. May 1937.

MSW 1.295–309. On practice. July 1937.

MSW 1.311–47. On contradiction. August 1937.

MSW 2.47–59. Interview with the British journalist James Bertram. October 1937.

MSW 2.195–211. The role of the Chinese Communist Party in the national war. October 1938.

MSW 2.213–17. The question of independence and initiative within the united front. November 1938.

MSW 2.237–39. The May 4th movement. May 1939.

MSW 2.241–49. The orientation of the youth movement. May 1939.

MSW 2.305–34. The Chinese revolution and the Chinese Communist Party. December 1939.

MSW 2.339–84. On new democracy. January 1940.

MSW 2.441–49. On policy. December 1940.

MSW 3. 11–13. Preface to 'Rural surveys'. March 1941.

MSW 3.69–98. Talks at the Yenan forum on literature and art. May 1942.

MSW 3.117–22. Some questions concerning methods of leadership. June 1943.

MSW 3.153–61. Get organised! November 1943.

MSW 3.177–225. Resolution on certain questions in the history of our Party. April 1945.

MSW 3.235–37. The united front in cultural work. October 1944.

MSW 3.255–320. On coalition government. April 1945.

MSW 3.321–24. The Foolish Old Man who removed the mountains. June 1945.

MSW 3.325–29. On production by the army and rectification. April 1945.

MSW 4.53–63. On the Chungking negotiations. October 1945.

MSW 4.181–89. On some important problems of the Party's present policy. January 1948.

MSW 4.197–99. Correct the 'Left' errors in land reform propaganda. February 1948.

MSW 4.361–75. Report to the second plenary session of the Seventh Central Committee of the Communist Party of China. March 1949.

MSW 4.411–24. On the people's democratic dictatorship. June 1949.

MSW 4.451–59. The bankruptcy of the idealist conception of history. September 1949.

MFE. Mao Tse-tung, Four essays on philosophy. Peking, 1966.

MFE 79–133. On the correct handling of contradictions among the people. February 1957.

MFE 134–36. Where do correct ideas come from? May 1963.

MQ. Quotations from Chairman Mao Tse-tung. Peking, 1967.

MQ 27–28. Speech at the Chinese Communist Party's national conference on propaganda work. March 1957.

MQ 40–41. Note on 'The seven well-written documents of Chekiang province concerning cadres' participation in physical labour'. May 1963.

MQ 118. Note to 'Surplus labour has found a way out'. 1955.

Mao Tse-tung and others

HE. More on the historical experience of proletarian dictatorship. December 1956.

PR. Peking Review (cited by year and number of issue).

PR 63–33. Mao Tse-tung, Statement in support of the American Negroes in their just struggle against racial discrimination by U.S. imperialism. August 8, 1963.

PR 66–33. Decision of the Central Committee of the Chinese

Communist Party concerning the great proletarian cultural revolution. August 12, 1966.

PR 66–38. Take firm hold of the revolution and stimulate production. *Renmin ribao* editorial. September 16, 1966.

PR 67–21. 6-9. Circular of the Central Committee of the Chinese Communist Party. May 16, 1966.

PR 67–21. 10–12. A great historic document. *Hongqi* and *Renmin ribao* editorial. May 19. 1967.

PR 68–14. Revolutionary committees are fine. *Renmin ribao, Hongqi,* and *Jiefangjun bao* editorial. April 5, 1968.

PR 69–18. Lin Piao, Report to the Ninth National Congress of the Communist Party of China. April 28, 1969.

PR 70–22. Mao Tse-tung, Peoples of the world, unite and defeat the U.S. aggressors and all their running-dogs. May 20, 1970.